THE LAW FIRM OF TOMORROW

from the makers of

rocket matter

ISBN: PENDING

First edition, December 2011

DISCLAIMER

We're happy to inject interesting ideas into legal business discourse. We believe those who open their minds to some of the concepts in the book will reap benefits of improved efficiency and profitability. This book contains a mix of facts, analysis, and opinions, and we hope readers find it thought provoking and helpful.

That said, though we believe the information meets that criteria, we assume no responsibility for errors or omissions, and do not warrant or guarantee accuracy, completeness, or appropriateness for any specific set of circumstances. Similarly, we take no responsibility for any websites, links or other content referred to, linked to, or suggested. Nothing in this book should be construed as, or a substitute for, legal or other professional advice.

WHAT IS ROCKET MATTER?

Rocket Matter is the leading web-based practice management and time and billing application for small to mid-size law firms.

When we launched in February of 2008, we were the first legal technology available for running a law firm online. We were surprised at the number of attorneys who immediately joined our service, looking to manage their matters, clients, and invoicing from any computer at anytime.

Since then, amazing mobile devices such as the iPhone , iPad, and Droid have transformed attorney access to information. In addition, the global economy had declined, putting new pressures on the operational efficiencies of law firms, and altering the make up of large, traditional law firms.

In that time, via the Rocket Matter product, our blogging, video, CLE, webinars, and contributions in legal trade publications, we've helped law firms navigate these new waters. We've introduced new ideas for marketing, operations, and technology to help legal professionals adapt to the ever-changing professional environment.

So please, enjoy this first installment of The Law Firm of Tomorrow, and become part of our cutting-edge community if you're not already! **Follow us, and spread the good word**!

Facebook   Twitter   YouTube   Podcast   Our Site

MARKETING 2.0

SMILING, HAPPINESS, AND HOW TO MAKE A GOOD FIRST IMPRESSION

You don't have to wait until the end of the year and holiday season to focus on achieving goals, improving yourself, and making resolutions.

I like to pretend every month is December and constantly think of my New Year's resolutions. I don't wait until January 1st, however, I implement change immediately. To that end, I frequently review some of the classic personal improvement books I've collected over the years. My favorite, by far, is the Dale Carnegie stuff.

How to Win Friends and Influence People

One of my favorite chapters from <u>How to Win Friends and Influence People</u> is, "A Simple Way to Make a Good First Impression." Making a good impression is a great skill for lawyers who are constantly looking for clients or referral sources. Although it's a cliché, you only get one crack at making a first impression. You're constantly networking, so you might as well do it to the best of your ability.

As Carnegie points out:

"The expression one wears on one's face is far more important than the clothes one wears on one's back. Charles Schwab told me his smile had been worth a million dollars. And he was probably understating the truth. For Schwab's personality, his charm, his ability to make people like him were almost wholly responsible for his extraordinary success; and one of the most delightful factors in his personality was his captivating smile."

One of the reasons people like dogs so much Carnegie points out, is that they freak out with happiness when we walk in the door after being gone for a while. It's a natural response to be glad to see them in return. Smiles serve the same function. When they're genuine smiles, not a forced, phony, s***-eating grin, the people you meet are happy to make your acquaintance.

Show Your Teeth

Smiling makes us happy, which Carnegie points out, is what everyone is seeking. He wrote in the 1930's what modern "happiness scientists" echo today:

"Happiness doesn't depend on outward conditions. It depends on inner conditions. It isn't what you have or who you are or where you are or what you are doing that makes you happy or unhappy. It is what you think about."

So show your teeth, stop complaining, and network effectively! As Carnegie points out in the following Chinese proverb: "A man without a smiling face must not open a shop."

EMAIL MARKETING: SURPRISING INSIGHT LAWYERS CAN USE

Email is one of the tools we use regularly to engage our own community. We periodically inform folks about our new features, our fun promotions, and other information that we think is valuable to our subscribers. We also put out a popular newsletter.

Email marketing is also a tactic that our lawyers and law firms are exploring more and more, especially given its relative low cost and - when done properly - good success rate.

The general topic of "email marketing" is massive, and there is no shortage of advice and information out there to review. Unfortunately a lot of email marketing literature is subjective: "unicorns and rainbows." It's often very high-level, "feel good" type advice.

The Science of Email Marketing

Our friends over at HubSpot took a different approach on the topic and addressed it in a more persuasive way: they went to the data.

In "The Science of Email Marketing", HubSpot looked at actual data - 9.5 billion emails from MailChimp, and discovered some very interesting - sometimes counterintuitive - facts. Dan Zarella offers up some data-driven conclusions concerning matters like the best day to send emails, the best time to send emails, whether to include links, and how often to send emails. Very cool stuff.

Also very counterintuitive. Get this: apparently email campaigns sent over the weekend have the best click-throughs!

We'd love for you to share your own experiences with email marketing - especially if you have a great tip or two. Are you email marketing to your clients? What kind of tactics have you tried? What worked - what didn't?

The Social Media Hangover, Legal Edition

D. Todd Smith, appellate lawyer / internet hipster / writer out of Texas, taps into the same vein of Internet overuse we saw a lot of in 2010 writing.

In his article for Texas Lawyer, also posted on JD Supra, How Lawyers Can Avoid Social Media Burnout, Smith echoes the growing fatigue many of us have with the overload of Tweets, Status Updates, and whatnot constantly streaming in at us. Smith writes:

How Much is Too Much?

Turn off notifications. Because of the sheer number of updates in almost any size network, social media can be even more distracting than e-mail when it comes to desktop notifications. Productivity experts like Timothy Ferriss, author of The 4-Hour Workweek, recommend turning off notifications and handling e-mails in batches no more than a few times per day. A lawyer should protect his/her sanity and stay on task by batching social media, as well.

When Facebook and Twitter started taking off in 2008 and 2009, users engaged in a mad scramble to embrace the networks, amass a bunch of followers/friends, and stay highly engaged. Now, as the dust begins to settle and we understand the utility of these tools, we have the opportunity to ask, "What have social networks done for me lately" and scale back activity accordingly.

If social networks are driving hordes of leads to your site, then by all means do whatever works for you. But if you've discovered diminishing returns with your activity and find it encroaching on aspects of your life, perhaps it's time to pull back the throttle a little. Resist the temptation to think you're doing something wrong, even if your consultant (I'm using that term mockingly) tells you that you are.

A kindred spirit with the folks here at Legal Productivity, Smith echoes in his article some of the things we've discussed here on this blog: email batching, unplugging, and deemphasizing your number of followers.

In our 24-7 gotta know everything and everybody world, this advice seems counterintuitive. But if you're approaching burnout, hangover, fatigue, call it what you will, give it a try.

CRITICAL FACEBOOK PRIVACY AND SECURITY CONSIDERATIONS

We all did stupid things in college, and now Facebook is there to help us broadcast those youthful indiscretions to the world. Even the founders of the social media juggernaut themselves have skeletons in their closets, including Eduardo Saverin's famous chicken cannibalism incident.

Not only that, there's all sorts of talk out there in the world, and now you're a professional with a reputation to manage. So what measures can you take when anyone you've ever known, at anytime, can post whatever they want about you to the online world?

If you don't know how to toggle these settings, we put together a three minute YouTube video that shows you how to adjust your Facebook privacy step-by-step.

Determine what you want to share.

The whole idea about Facebook is about exchanging information with your friends and/or colleagues. So step one is to clarify what you're comfortable sharing and with whom. Do you care if strangers see pictures of your kids? How about everyone in your network? Are you cool with random people putting up pictures of you and tagging you in them?

Conduct your Facebook sessions over HTTPS.

Make sure that all use of Facebook is over an encrypted channel. In the spirit of knowing who you're sharing information with, make sure that other people at Starbucks, the library, or whatever other WiFi spot you hop on won't be able to see your Facebook traffic.

Get Notified When People Talk About You

I recommend setting notifications for when people tag you in anything. You're going to want to know if there's a new photo, video, or post involving you.

Ensure Only You Can See Your Tagged Photos or Videos

When someone tags you in a photo or video, you can configure Facebook to let **only you** see the tag. This is a pretty important feature for maintaining your reputation. When others have the ability to broadcast images of you to the rest of the world, you cede a lot of reputation control.

We're interested. What are your favorite settings for Facebook privacy and security?

FACEBOOK FOR LAW FIRMS PART I: 3 TIPS

For many of us, understanding how to use a blog to drive business on the web is clear. Using Twitter, well, unless you're an über-genius it probably took a while to understand how to incorporate that into your practice, but you got it eventually.

But Facebook? How can your business benefit from Overlord Zuckerberg's monstrous creation?

Twitter and Blogging are pretty much one-trick ponies. But Facebook has a whole slew of features, not to mention the trickiness of blending personal information with work information. In this series, we'll explore how Facebook can be used as a tool in your marketing belt - without a trip to the disciplinary board.

We at Rocket Matter, are working through a Facebook marketing strategy for our own web-based legal practice management software and our goal is to share what we've learned and what's worked for us so far. And let's get one thing straight: nobody pays us for social media expertise. It's not a service we provide. So what you're reading here is the straight dope about what works for us and what doesn't.

Understand the Difference Between Facebook Pages and Groups

When representing your law firm on Facebook, you can choose to create a "Page" or a "Group". They are different in a couple of minor but key ways.

Groups allow you to directly send messages to your members' inboxes. Pages allow you to send something called "Updates", which aren't immediately accessible from your notifications widget. They don't pop up at you - you have to do a little digging. This is what receiving an Update looks like. Note the navigation on the left which shows you how I got to the screen.

Members of a group can also easily invite their friends, allowing the group to grow quickly.

Groups, however, don't allow you to have a purty little URL like http://www.facebook.com/Rocket.Matter. You get a big, long, ugly URL with a randomly generated number. Pages also allow some additional flexibility with functionality - additional apps can be used. On our page, for example, we include the JD Supra app to list our shared documents. Both Pages and Groups allow for discussions on the Wall, or by starting discussion threads.

For more information on this topic, take a look at Facebook Group vs Facebook Fan Page: What's Better?, and take a look at the comments, which include some key corrections and great information.

My personal opinion? Unless you're trying for a big viral play, which is probably unlikely for a small law firm, stick with a Fan Page and start from there. But I would love to hear differing opinions if you have one.

Create Exclusive Content for your Facebook Page

You have a wall, events, and other ways to engage folks who've been nice enough to like your page. Use these tools! Engage your fans and treat them well. Offer them things they can't get in any other way. The Harvard Business Review profiled this strategy of "participatory promotion" employed by Lowes:

Lowes ran a Black Friday campaign on Facebook in which it offered a limited number of items at ridiculously low prices for fans only. Most discounts were in the range of 90% and were limited to the first 100 people to check out with the item at lowes.com. Not only did this engage existing customers, but it drove new customers to "like" Lowes' Facebook page, allowing Lowes to post future deals on their newsfeeds.

Use Your Wall and Engage Your Fans

Personally, I'm not a big believer of linking Tweets to Facebook status updates. I tend to unfriend or de-like entities that engage in this practice, which come off as spammy IMOSHO (in my oh-so humble opinion). When I see hashtags on Facebook, I run screaming. Rather, craft a couple of unique things for your Facebook page.

Example: post your latest blog post, which you also do on Twitter, but perhaps give it a different sentence or two introduction when it goes on your wall. That slight differentiation goes a long way. Respond to comments, always, just like you would on your blog.

Share cool content. The nice thing about sharing videos or content you enjoy on your Facebook page as opposed to Twitter is its staying power. Content is presented in little bite-size overviews, making it easily consumable, and by virtue more valuable.

One last thought for now: people are consuming Facebook content in different ways. A new breed of iPad apps, led by Flipboard, present social media content in a slick, magazine-like format. People are on Facebook, and if you want to get in front of them, you need to be there too.

FACEBOOK FOR LAW FIRMS PART II: 3 MORE TIPS

In this series, *How To Use Facebook For Law Firms*, we explore how your law firm can benefit from Overlord Zuckerberg's monstrous creation. In Part One, we discussed exclusive content, pages and groups, and engagement. This is Part Two. Get ready. It's hot.

Take a look at Page Insights.

From the main view of your law firm Fan Page, click "View Insights". This takes you to a handy graph that shows usage and visitation patterns for your Facebook fiefdom. The data is not particularly rich: you can see the number of Users and Interactions (likes and comments) plotted over time. Week and month views are provided.

In spite of the limited information, one thing you can certainly measure is growth (or shrinkage) over time. Fans of Google Analytics will feel right at home.

Watch Your Post Frequency

I have one word for you if you funnel your Twitter account into your Facebook page status update: you're burying the world with Facebook spam. No only that, the hashtags and little '@' signs make it seem like alien species, like the boa constrictors invading the Everglades down here in Florida.

Even if you're not using Twitter and posting on your Fan page all of the time, you risk annoying your fans, who may end up deciding to hide all of your messages. And Facebook makes it easy if you don't want to endure someone's fire hose of information. Not to pick on my friend Niki, but if I wanted to make her stuff invisible it's quite easy. You click on the X by her post and *voilá*, it's gone!

Employ Apps

Switching up the tabs and functionality you can add to your Facebook page can differentiate yourself and make your page more of a destination. It can also help you assemble various pieces of your online life. For example, on the Rocket Matter page, we added the JD Supra app so that our documents are easily listed.

Questions is another great app for law firms to employ. Much as the name suggests, Questions allows you to send out little poll questions to your friends. These quizzes are always fun to take, are certainly interactive, and can raise your brand profile.

In March, Facebook added the ability for companies to embed their own content into a Facebook fan page via something called iframes (this is not a Facebook invention, it is a standard web widget). Setting up your own content within a Facebook iframe may be a little tricky for some to figure out. Take a look at this tutorial and make a judgement call. Someone with computer knowledge, even a kid in the high-school computer club or a university intern could help out inexpensively.

WHAT YOUR TWITTER FOLLOWER STATS MEAN

To anyone on Twitter: raise your hand if you don't pay attention to your number of followers. No matter how not vain you claim to be, your follower number is something that tugs oh-so-gently at your consciousness.

To those using Twitter for a while, it becomes obvious that you can quickly increase your followers in one of two ways:

1) Become incredibly famous.

2) Follow as many other people as you can, banking on people following you in return.

The Reciprocity Pitfall

Since most people are not incredibly famous, they seek to build up their followers and choose option #2: they follow a bunch of people they never intend to pay attention to. A lot of people will reciprocate and follow you, even though they never intend to pay any attention to you in return. Building up the number of followers in this way works for the most part.

However, this potentially leaves you in the position of following more people than follow you. When grossly out of proportion, the follower to followee ratio speaks poorly of a Tweep, since it tends to indicate intention of using Twitter as principally a broadcast medium. In other words, if someone follows way more people than are following him/her, that person may be perceived by some as a Twitter parasite.

Influencers

On the other hand, if individuals have more people following them than they follow, they tend to be perceived as Twitter bad-asses. They're seen as influencers, adding to the dialog and serving as positive, upstanding members of the community.

Hence the strategy employed by some Tweeps: they follow as many people as possible to get as many followers as possible, then they un-follow those same folks to keep their ratio balanced. Gotta keep up those Twitter appearances!

But aside from the cachet of having a big fat number of followers for your Twitter, what's the real value of having a lot of people following you? Are they really listening to you? In terms of getting your message out, does it make a difference if you have 100, 200, 10,000, or 100,000 followers?

From Follow to Lead

The data may surprise you. According to inbound marketing firm Hubspot, in their 2009 paper The State of Inbound Lead Generation, returns diminish once you cross the threshold of several hundred followers. Leads increase dramatically between companies with no followers and then several hundred, but beyond 500, the leads actually decrease.

According to Hubspot's analysis, "Customers with large numbers of followers are probably attracting viewers who are exclusively interested in the content."

Either that, or they're attracting viewers that follow them blindly in return for a stat-building follow. ;-)

LEGAL BLOGGERS: GETTING YOUR CONTENT SCRAPED? FIGHT BACK!

"Once your Internet footprint reaches a certain size, chances are people will start scraping your content." Link.

As anyone who went to law school knows, it's important to cite your sources. For example, note the quotation marks, and the fact that the above is hyperlinked for proper online citation format.

In an academic setting, failure to properly cite can give rise to charges of plagiarism. In a court room, it robs one's argument of authority. On the Internet, however, it would seem that it's a shortcut to page hits and google-ad dollars.

In fact, "ctrl-c-ctrl-v-ing" someone else's blogged content has even been given a new moniker to go along with its new arena: Content Scraping.

Content scraping

Content scraping is an obvious copyright violation, but, if one writes well and often enough, as the introductory quote from blogger Eileen Smith's post about dealing with the fallout of being 'scraped' indicates, it becomes a fact of life online.

So, what's a legal content producer to do?

Here's some options, 'curated' from the interwebs:

Cease-and-desist 'em

The most direct way to stop content scraping is to contact the scraper via a cease and desist email. The online anti-graphic redistribution group R.I.G.H.T.S has a <u>model cease and desist email on their website</u> (and it's free to use).

The advantage of a cease and desist approach is that you only have to do it once your rights have been violated, and it's a familiar process. If you're a first-time scraping victim, this is probably a good first step at getting back control of your content. You know who has stolen your work, so you ask them to take it down or else. As a legal writer, you're probably familiar with the process of backing up a cease and desist email with follow-up communications and/or service of process should the offending content not be removed in a reasonably prompt fashion.

The disadvantage to the cease and desist approach comes when you're no longer dealing with a single or small group of content scrapers. When you're attacked by piranhas, you can't kill them one at a time. That's when you need to move on to more technical solutions.

'Tag' your content and set up Google Alerts to monitor its life-cycle

A second level approach to combating content theft is to tag your content with unlikely phrasing, and then set a Google Alert for that phrase. This is akin to the way Monsanto tags its seeds. For example, in the course of writing an article on, say, the tax implications of declaring a dividend, find a quote from Learned Hand that anchors a point that you're making. Try and place that quote 'tag' deep into the body of your article or post, to avoid it being excised along with the headline or lead, if the content scraper is savvy enough to attempt cosmetic alterations to avoid the Google Alert approach. Then, set the Google Alert, and you've essentially created a sonar system that will ping you back whenever someone has used your content, and then cease-and-desist them.

Creative Commons

Another approach to content rights management is publishing your content under a Creative Commons license. You can read about Creative Commons as a philosophical approach to the Internet's copyright ecology here. But, to put it simply, Creative Commons is a way to allow people to repurpose your content within certain bounds, and is respected by content producers and distributors as an adaptation of copyright to a virtual environment that facilitates and is, itself, dependent upon socialized dissemination of information. This choice allows your work to get greater exposure, and directs re-purposers to give credit to you, the original author.

Join a clearinghouse, once they're up and running

A step-up from Creative Commons, and an approach that directly monetizes your shared content, is the clearinghouse. A clearinghouse is essentially a name brand creative commons for professional writers. In a clearinghouse regime, your content is placed in what has come to be called a digital 'wrapper'. That wrapper contains information about where the content came from. It also communicates with the clearinghouse itself, registering impressions or click-throughs, or however else that content is licensed to the content distributor who picked it out of the clearinghouse inventory.

The clearinghouse acts as a middleman of sorts, billing the distributors and paying out to the producers based upon that licensing agreement.

The advantages of this approach to content producers is obvious, as the clearinghouse does the monitoring, enforcement, and billing for the producers. Also, being registered with a clearinghouse as a content producer is, itself, a form of marketing for the content producer, as such will distinguish a content producer from the crowd.

The disadvantage is that the clearinghouse approach isn't exactly in existence yet, but that will change very soon. The Associated Press has a system that they report will be up soon, and Martin C. Langeveld of Circlabs reports that Mizzou is developing one as well:

"I'm working with Randy Smith and other faculty from the Journalism School, Law School, Computer Science and Agricultural Economics to study the emerging clearinghouse systems designed to govern an orderly exchange of news content under commonly accepted rights and payments protocols. These systems will be enabled by tagging systems already developed and deployed, and in addition to the rather small revenue opportunity created by deterring unauthorized re-publication, they will create transformative new opportunities for content to find a wider audience and for publishers to deliver a richer mix of content to their audiences."

Anti-Crawl and its discontents

In the meantime, I'd like to steer you away from Anti-Crawl and other content-tagging software. Based upon my research, it looks like these solutions are awkward, easily evaded and often over-priced (though Anti-Crawl offers a free script to start out with). The guerilla approach of self-tagging with quotations or phraseology accomplishes the same goal without the cost, and, as a legal professional, you're in a position to handle most content scraping situations with an email with electronic letterhead. Nobody wants to get into a paperwork war with a lawyer.

LEGAL
TECH SAVVINESS

MOBILE SECURITY CHECKLIST FOR ATTORNEYS

I recently had the honor of <u>writing a piece for ILTA's Peer to Peer magazine on mobile security</u> and presenting a webinar on the same topic. One piece of research blew me away: in a six-month period in Chicago, over 20 THOUSAND (yes - THOUSAND) cell phones were left in taxis.

Sure, *maybe* Chicago's taxi seats are stickier than most, and perhaps the cold forces people into taxis more than in, say, Boca Raton, FL. The point is, you're apt to lose a phone.

And these days, with large amounts of data storage, functionality, and computational power on these things, that spells trouble for attorneys protecting client data.

How to keep your smartphone data safe:

Remote Wiping

Consider having the ability to destroy data from a distance. Larger law firms can employ solutions like Blackberry Enterprise Server or Good For Enterprise. If you have an iPhone, a simple MobileMe plan can do the trick.

Use Password Lock

You have no excuse not to set your phone to lock automatically after 15 minutes of idle activity. This tech is adopted by all small smartphone makers in one form or another. Use a code to unlock the phone and set the phone to destroy data if the wrong passcode is entered 10 times.

Use Web Applications for Sensitive Data

Instead of cradle-synching apps where data is saved both on the desktop and the mobile, consider using web apps that deliver information wirelessly. You'll find it easier to stay in synch, but more importantly, a simple logout will keep the information from falling into the wrong hands.

Know Wifi Rules

Make sure if you're connecting to a public WiFi spot at Starbucks, Panera, or the courthouse that any sensitive data is viewed over 128-bit encryption. A web app can do this if you notice the browser connecting over the "https" protocol.

Don't Over-App

Some apps, such as Dropbox, enable you to work with data stored on another computer. These apps are potential security holes, since a malicious party would be able to gain access to this data via your mobile. Make sure you're aware of the apps you download and what they give exposure to.

Also, if you're in the Wild West of the Google App Android marketplace, only download apps you know can be trusted, since there's no verification that those apps are not malicious.

Standardize:

Get everyone on the same page. Make sure everyone in your organization is aware of mobile security risks and adheres to the same policies. Remember that a chain is only as strong as its weakest link.

ONLINE PRIVACY CONSIDERATIONS FOR LAWYERS TO PONDER

When I discuss my privacy concerns with people, frequently the response I get is, "If you're not doing anything wrong, why do you care?"

I'll tell you why I care. Just because something's private doesn't mean it's bad or sinister. Example: When I take a shower in the morning, that's private. I don't want anyone else seeing that. The love two people share is a private matter. My innermost thoughts, hopes, fears, and ambitions, I only share with those closest to me. Not for the world.

And legal professionals, more than most, should be attuned to online privacy concerns due to their sensitivity to attorney client privilege. Which is why, as someone who runs an online legal practice management company , I stew and fume when I see egregious violations of someone's online privacy.

Privacy Concerns

Two recent privacy concerns that should grab your attention. First is a headline in the New York Times that the federal government wants better hooks into private companies' telecom technology for better snooping. The piece from October 18th, states under the big banner headline "U.S. Pushes to Ease Technical Obstacles to Wiretapping":

"The disclosure that the administration is seeking ways to increase pressure on carriers already subject to the 1994 law comes less than a month after The New York Times reported on a related effort: a plan to bring Internet companies that enable communications — like Gmail, Facebook, BlackBerry and Skype — under the law's mandates for the first time, a demand that would require major changes to some services, technical designs, and business models."

Then there was the recent disclosure in the Wall Street Journal that app creators for Facebook, notably the people who create FarmVille, are sharing your personal information harvested from the social media site. Apparently, users willingly accept the wholesale collection of their personal Facebook information in return for the almost irresistible allure of growing virtual carrots. These companies, in violation of Facebook code, were sharing user identifiers with other companies.

Remember, it's Facebook's profile on you, not your profile on Facebook. Do you really want random companies knowing who you associate with?

What Your Data Says About You

More data can be pieced together with Facebook info than you realize. In fact, MIT computer scientists were able to predict which Facebook users were gay, even though they hadn't revealed that information on their site. Read about 'Project Gaydar'. NOT COOL.

You as the consumer MUST be aware of the equitable exchange of information: what are you willing to give up in order to get what you want? Your privacy is more precious than you may or may not realize. Take steps to defend it, and understand who you're getting into bed with when you conduct business online.

5 STEPS TO KILLER INEXPENSIVE PHONE SYSTEMS

Remember when you needed a consultant and a $10,000 phone system for your small law office? If you're not up to speed on the latest and greatest in Internet telephony, those days are over.

For $52 a month, a two person law office can hook themselves up with a large-firm telephone presence. Two major technology advances paved the way for this revolution, namely, hosted PBX systems and computer-based calling via Skype.

Skype

In addition to allowing video chat, screen sharing, instant messaging, and Skype-to-Skype calling, you can purchase an online Skype number for $6 a month, allowing you to receive incoming calls. The latter is key to the setup I'm describing, so the first thing you'll need is a Skype account with your own telephone number.

The second thing you'll need is what's known as a Virtual PBX system. PBX, which stands for "Private branch exchange", is a business telephone system which allows for extensions, transferring calls, out-of-office messages, phone queues, and other functionality.

Phone.com, Grasshopper, and Phone Booth are all examples of virtual PBX systems.

With a PBX system, you'll be able to have callers dial your law firm and receive a message like the following: "Welcome to the Jones, Bierko, and Hill law firm. You may dial the extension of your party at any time. To speak with someone about the status of your case, press 1. To inquire about a new case, press 2," or something to that effect.

Armed with this knowledge, here's what you need to do to set up a phone system for your small law office:

1) **Sign up for Skype**, and make sure you choose an online number. It doesn't matter what this number is, because the only party interested in your Skype number is your Virtual PBX system.

2) **Take a look at Phone.com**, Phone Booth, and Grasshopper, and choose a Virtual PBX system that matches the features you want. You may want to purchase a 1-800 number or port an existing one over. This is usually very inexpensive, below $20.00.

3) **Create some extensions in your PBX**, and point them to the corresponding Skype numbers. You may also want to set up some call-handling rules, based on your software's capabilities, such as how long to ring your Skype number before leaving voicemail. Here's a screenshot of my extension setup:

4) **Record messages for the various PBX functions**. You'll need voicemail. You'll need a closed message, a welcome message, and a "transferring" message when someone dials an extension or selects a category in the phone tree.

Recordings can be professionally done, and most computers have built-in capabilities to record audio. If this is something you need help with, either a) find a tech savvy high-school kid in your neighborhood with a Mac to give you a hand or b) the PBX service might be able to recommend voice talent for you.

5) **Tweak**. It doesn't take too long to get most of this stuff set up, but you'll want to test the different flows and tighten them up. Remember, your phone system is a visible exterior of your law firm. Make it pretty.

REPORT: LEGAL CLOUD COMPUTING IS THE CORNERSTONE OF LAW 2.0

A paper called "Law 2.0: Intelligent Architecture for Transactional Law" from University of Colorodo's Silicon Flatirons Roundtable Series on Entrepreneurship has some of the deepest, hard-hitting thinking you'll come across concerning the present and future state of lawyers, their clients, and the technology changing the industry.

Props to Jason Mendelson for blogging about the article and for his contributions to the roundtable. One of the more hotly debated aspects of law in recent years is the commoditization of services, brought to the forefront of consciousness by Richard Susskind's book *The End of Lawyers,* and 2009 keynote address at ABA Techshow.

In a graphic worthy of the infographic site "Chart Porn", Mendelson offers a matrix describing which aspects of law lend themselves more towards commoditization and which ones don't. (Fig. 3)

In addition, one of the key drivers enabling Law 2.0 is Cloud Computing, states the report. Cloud Computing write the authors, "Enabled by "(1) increased broadband connectivity; (2) larger and cheaper storage; and (3) faster and cheaper processing, is increasingly trusted by lawyers and will become an increasingly more important component of legal tech."

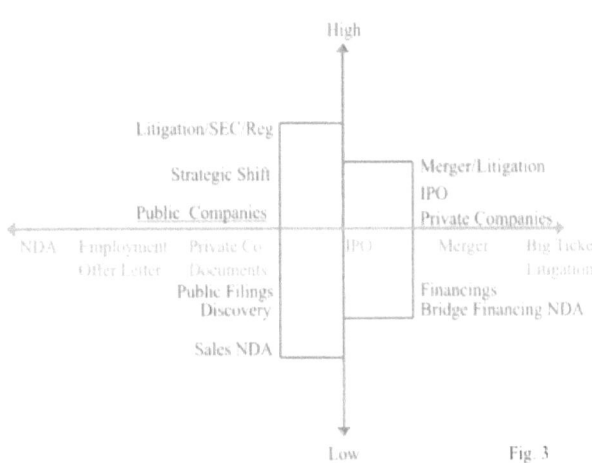

Fig. 3

The above matrix describes which aspects of law lend themselves more towards commoditization (Above the X access) and which ones don't (Below the X access)

8 Ways Using Online Law Practice Management Software Will Make You Sound Like Your Old Man

"When I was a kid I used to walk uphill to school. Five miles. Both ways!" Hearing the old war stories of one's parents is part of life.

If you're like me, you're probably already engaging in similar dribble with your children: "When I was a kid, we couldn't see our photos instantly. We used to have to take them to a camera store and wait a week!" Or: "When I was a kid, we couldn't pause T.V.".

So, as lawyers now have amazing new technologies like online law practice management software, the business of law is made much easier. Here's how attorneys who've adopted such solutions might sound to junior associates of the future:

1) **When I was a junior associate**, we didn't have one consolidated database. Everybody ran Outlook and we were constantly out of synch. When a client came in, we each had to enter the client information 5 times! And if I entered the information incorrectly, my paralegal would bloody my knuckles.

2) **When I was a junior associate**, we didn't have fancy electronic message taking. We used to use these things called "pink message pads!" I would buy a dozen of them and a knish on my way to the movies for a quarter.

3) **When I was a junior associate**, we couldn't access our matters from any computer anywhere. We had to log into our

computers at work using Citrix. Or Remote Desktop. And that's if we were lucky!

4) **When I was a junior associate**, we couldn't run invoicing in a couple of minutes. We had to shut the whole firm down for a day or two, go through our notes, calendars, and build up our invoices from scratch. In five feet of snow!

5) **When I was a junior associate**, we couldn't just get new information on our smartphones over the air. We had these things called cradles, and you'd actually have to plug the smartphone into the computer! And gas was a nickel!

6) **When I was a junior associate**, we didn't instantly call up our files on the computer. We had these huge things called filing cabinets where we put all the paper. It took 15 minutes just to find what you're looking for, and that's if you were lucky. And you didn't deserve to call yourself an attorney if you didn't lose at lease two fingers in a filing cabinet accident.

7) **When I was a junior associate**, we couldn't just click someone's telephone number and initiate a phone call. We had to look it up in Outlook, then dial it on the phone, and you never knew if you had to dial a 'one' or the area code. And half the time, you'd electrocute yourself.

8) **When I was a junior associate**, we didn't have the calendar integrated with the contact manager integrated with the matters integrated with documents integrated with what you had for goldarned lunch. We had all that stuff in different pieces and had to tape it all together. And it broke 5 times a year and we'd have to pay some guy with greasy hair and a Star Wars t-shirt to come out and fix it!

7 Things to Know about Legal Cloud Computing

This much is clear: the Cloud is here to stay. Rocket Matter is currently celebrating three years of its initial launch (with a cool video). Leading vendors got together and formed theLegal Cloud Computing Association. The talk atLegalTech New York this year was not about Cloud's potential, but it's realization.

What do law firms need to know about the Cloud? There's enough information to fill an entire day-long seminar. But this quick, seven point guide should point you in the right direction.

1) Cloud software is software you access over the Internet.

The term "Cloud" itself is a murky one, and the IBM commercials where they feature a bunch of brainiacs talking about the Cloud only confuses the issue. All you really need to know is that Cloud software is accessed over the Internet, using a browser like Firefox or via an app from the iTunes store or Droid Marketplace.

2) Cloud software can be accessed from any device.

Well, any device with an Internet connection, that is. Good Cloud software is usable from Macs or PCs without you being able to tell the difference, and they should also include ways of using the software from iPads, Droids, iPhones, or other mobile devices.

3) So far, bar ethics opinions are cool with responsible Cloud usage.

Not all bar associations have weighed in: North Carolina is, as of this writing, reviewing the issue and the ABA is also looking at legal Cloud computing as part of their 20/20 Ethics Commission. That said, Alabama and New York have paved the way, saying that lawyers should take reasonable steps to ensure client confidentiality. We will explore "reasonable steps" in later blog posts.

4) Not all Cloud providers are created equal.

As state bar associations point out, lawyers should perform due diligence to understand if their client communication and billing data is safe. All communication to the Cloud server, for example, should be encrypted under at least 128-bit SSL encryption, servers must be *physically* secure under lock and key, backups should routinely be provided, and a customer should be able to retrieve their data for portability. A sample set of standards is available for download here.

5) You should be able to get your data from your Cloud provider, and it should be usable.

Per that last point, you need to be able to get your data if you need it, and the terms of service should specify that the data is yours. First of all, for your own peace of mind, it's nice to know you can get your critical data when you need it. Second of all, should you decide to leave your software provider, you're going to want to take your history with you. Thanks to vCard and ICS, standards exist to transport contact and calendar records, respectively. For more freeform data, you're going to want to make sure you get it in spreadsheet form, not some sort of bizarre proprietary format.

6) Using the Cloud may be more secure than your current setup.

Are you sending confidential information over unencrypted email? You might as well publish it on a billboard. Yet for some reason, it's okay with ethics rules to do so. Information stored or communicated via good Cloud software is encrypted over a minimum 128-bit channel.

Also, how is your data physically stored? Who has access to your computers with sensitive information - landlords, cleaning staff? With responsible Cloud providers, your data is under lock and key with 24-7 surveillance. And considering that data theft is 10 times more likely to be physical than via a high-tech cyber attack, physical security is your number one enemy when it comes to a data breach.

7) Cloud software is easier to maintain than desktop software.

The days of upgrades are over for Cloud consumers. With web-based software, the applications simply update themselves, no IT support needed. Also, since features tend to be pared down on the web, the software tends not to be as complex, nor does it bloat or slow down over time. Adding users is also easier, since you don't need additional client installs or have to worry about introducing their installation into the network.

If you want to read more, check out the this resource kit featuring a half-dozen articles I've written for legal technology periodicals.

3 WAYS PRACTICE MANAGEMENT SOFTWARE HELPS LAW FIRMS

Duct Tape! That's what's holding together law office technology at the typical small firm (metaphorically speaking, that is). Typically the duct tape holds together Outlook for contacts, calendar, and email, Quickbooks for billing, and I don't even want to know what Word doc or other rigged solution firms have to track the progress on a case.

Don't take it from me. Talk to any of the North America's Practice Management Advisors, or PMA's. They'll tell you to take a good hard look at legal practice management software. Here's three reasons how an LPM system help:

1) Less Duplication = Less Errors

What you want to avoid: every computer keeping a separate repository of contacts and documents. Everyone in the firm should have access to the same data. When you update a contact once, it updates everywhere. Seems simple, but a lot of people don't do it.

Also, when you set up or update client information, if you're entering information in five different software programs, you're not only wasting time, you're introducing a high risk for data entry error.

2) On-time, Accurate Billing

Getting consistently accurate bills out on time is, in my opinion, one of the most important operational aspect of any law firm. The reasons for this are many, including improved cash flow, better client relations, and less work lost or written off. <u>We explore the underestimated importance of timely billing in earlier blog posts</u>.

Good legal practice management software, especially when integrated with time and billing software, eliminates the need for firms to scramble through calendar appointments and legal pads to try to reconstruct time. Less time is lost, the clients receive accurate and timely bills, and the firm machinery keeps operating efficiently.

3) More Efficient Time Management

Once all of your contact, calendar, and case information is organized in one easy-to-access place, you'll spend less time filing, less time paying someone else to file, and less time trying to figure out where information is. In addition, you won't need to spend time switching between programs, trying to move data from one program to another.

In addition, if you have lots of moving pieces organizing your law firm, you stand an increased chance of one of 'em going down.

Ultimately, legal practice management software is all about streamlining how you do business.

BECOMING A LEGAL BUSINESS HIPSTER

Engagement Vows, Part I: The New Client

One of the very first things that lawyers do when they start working with a new client is put together an engagement letter. It's critically important to have written engagement terms in place, and it is also ethically required.

Sample engagement letters are easy to find, and they usually satisfy basic ethical requirements, but they're often short on covering some of the practical day-to-day issues that can have a direct impact on the overall success of the relationship.

Explicitly addressing a few additional terms at the start of the engagement - adding a few "vows" - can help clarify expectations and set the relationship up for a positive start.

Here are five vows that a lawyer could elicit from a client at the start of the relationship, in addition to the "standard" engagement letter terms:

Client Vow #1:

"I promise to tell you the truth, the whole truth, and nothing but the truth – and to do so before we're in open court or signing contracts at a closing table."

The client needs to understand the nature and scope of the attorney-client relationship and to clearly understand the potential consequences of misrepresenting or withholding information from the attorney. Even innocent errors ("I didn't know that mattered") can be terribly damaging.

While the attorneys need to ask their clients the *right* questions, clients (especially those unfamiliar with the process at hand) need to appreciate the importance of providing open, complete communication to their counsel.

Client Vow #2:

"I promise to respect our agreed-upon communication protocols – i.e. I won't call you every hour, on the hour."

The client needs to makes sure that his or her advocate is well informed. However, that doesn't translate calling the office umpteen times a day, supplemented by hourly e-mail manifestos.

"Mr. Ptolemy called again - something about the universe revolving around him - he doesn't understand why you can't just call him back."

Discussing and setting down a reasonable communication plan can not only help ensure that everyone stays informed, it can also go a long way toward minimizing everyone's frustrations. Specifics will always vary - every lawyer has h/her own style, and every situation is different - but talking about this issue up front is important to properly set expectations. What constitutes an "emergency"? When can I normally expect a call back or e-mail reply? What about weekends and holidays? These are questions worthy of some up-front clarification.

Client Vow #3:

"I promise that we will always treat each other, and each other's team, respectfully."

Law offices are not exactly life-or-death hospital trauma centers, but they are nonetheless places where several complicated, important things happen simultaneously - many of which are subject to pressing deadlines. In a small law office, someone who answers the phone (if it's not lawyers themselves!) may be directly working on those things when a client calls, making sure everything is processed professionally and on time.

If that person can't immediately deal with your (non-urgent) issue, don't interpret it as a sly attempt to disrespect you, or an implication that your matter isn't important.

The same applies to other clients when they call and the law office is working directly on *your* matter. So, please, be polite. Be professional. It's just bad practice to be rude or short with the lawyer's team.

In addition, aside from being impolite, being snotty to an admin or paralegal is poor strategy. I distinctly remember one particularly sunny Saturday morning when I spotted an admin and a paralegal in the firm's office. Envisioning an exciting M&A deal, or maybe an emergency TRO in progress, I asked them what was up. "No rush" they said, "We just know next week is going to be crazy so we wanted to finish up some stuff for 'Mr. Smith' so he didn't have to wait. He's just such a nice man." When it comes to people skills, your grandma knew what she was talking about.

Client Vow #4:

I promise to carefully listen to your advice and, if I'm smart, follow it.

When the lawyer takes the time to explain a strategy or a particular tactic listen to him or her. Actively. Take notes (if necessary, the lawyer will tell you how to protect those notes). Ask questions. Take the time to familiarize yourself with the issues at hand. Ask for advice, and when your attorney gives it - think long and hard before you disregard it.

If you find yourself regularly disagreeing with the advice that your attorney is giving you, or if your attorney has proven to be neglectful or incompetent, then you need a different lawyer.   Those who have gone through more than two or three lawyers might consider investing in a psychologist instead.

Remind the client that they should not go through the trouble of searching for the right lawyers, finding them, engaging them, thoroughly working on a matter together, paying them, and then ignoring or otherwise failing to follow through on their advice.

Client Vow #5:

I promise to remember that you are the lawyer, and that I hired you to represent me.

A twist on "I promise to listen", a client must clearly understand that, once engaged, the lawyer is on point.   The lawyer has the requisite skill and experience to manage the matter, notwithstanding:

(a) what the client saw yesterday on: The People's Court, Judge Judy, Judge Joe Brown, Judge Mathis, Divorce Court;

(b) what the client's brother-in-law read last night on Wikipedia (or was it from some site called The Onion?, not sure ...) or

(c) what "ProSe4U" or "AlmstALwyr" said to the client when she was chatting with them, even though they both swore they got As in their undergrad pre-law classes.

Further, the client must promise not to write separate letters to the judge, post status updates about the matter on Facebook, try to "friend" the mediator who is mediating the proceeding, post (what the client thought were) anonymous messages attacking opposing counsel on public message boards, give spontaneous interviews about the matter to the media, or decide to secretly hire another attorney in a separate state to sue the exact same cause of action simultaneously, in a different forum (I have witnessed colleagues deal with four of those exact things).

Any action that involves the matter must be cleared by, or coordinated with, your attorney.

Soon, we'll look at some additional, "non-standard" vows that a lawyer can consider making to a client.

In the meantime, what other vows (that don't regularly appear in a standard engagement letter) would you suggest that your client make to you at the start of an engagement?

ENGAGEMENT VOWS, PART II: THE NEW CLIENT'S LAWYER

Previously, we took a look at 5 non-traditional "vows" that clients can make to their attorneys at the start of an engagement - promises that don't usually appear in a standard engagement letter. Today, we'll consider a few non-traditional vows the lawyer can make to a client.

Lawyer Vow #1:

I promise to always give you a complete, honest assessment of your matter – including prospects for success and realistic estimates of both anticipated costs–to–resolution and time frames for results.

Back when I practiced law, I worked with a smart, extremely wealthy client who'd get angry fast. He'd go off on grandiose tirades and would dream up highly sophisticated commercial litigation strategies. About 5% of the time, he'd offer up something completely legitimate and brilliant. The rest of the time, I could comfortably (and quickly) dismiss his theories as utterly ridiculous.

Facing reality early is usually the best way to solve any problem, legal or otherwise. Nobody does anyone any favors by constantly planning on the emergence of "best case" scenarios, playing "yes man", or letting the client hold onto unrealistic expectations. This is particularly true in litigated matters, when clients often envision aggressively litigating (nominally "for the principle") with very little appreciation for the actual speed of the process, the time and work required in motion practice and discovery, and the sometimes arbitrary nature of actual results.

Lawyer Vow #2:

"I will ensure that we communicate regularly."

The corollary: When I promise you a call-back, a draft of a document, or a meeting at a particular time or within a certain time frame, I will honor it.

Emergencies happen, but true emergencies are rare, and in those cases the lawyer should do everything possible to make certain the client's matter is well handled and that the client's personal time and plans are respected.

When clients see that their lawyers reliably *do* keep their word (and *vice-versa*), it's amazing how communication frustrations - frequently involving too many calls or too many emails - can magically decline.

Lawyer Vow #3:

When you ask me for advice, I will give a clear, concise recommendation.

Somewhere along the line, some professionals start changing from trusted advisors into just option generators.

Mike: "Thanks doc, I understand the options, what do you think I should do?"

Dr. Milquetoast: "You can choose to do any one of those things I just detailed."

Mike: "Got it, but based on your experience, your professional judgment, your knowledge of me, what do you think is the best course?"

Dr. Milquetoast: "It's really your decision, everyone is different."

Mike: "What would you do if you were me?"

Dr. Milquetoast: "Well, I can't really say because I'm not you."

When I engage a lawyer, I want the lawyer to draw upon his or her knowledge and experience to analyze the situation and give me a recommendation. I understand when things are my decision, and I want to be talked through the various options and nuances. However, I want my counsel to take a stand.

Lawyer Vow #4:

I will provide you with timely, detailed bills.

Yes, this isn't really "non-standard" - all engagement letters must contain a sufficiently detailed description of the billing process. However, this particular "vow" is a little more than that.

As a consumer of legal services, I can say there are few worse feelings than getting a new bill from a lawyer that relates to work performed about the time when "Eight Is Enough" was a top-rated TV show.

Getting a big bill is bad (and should really *never* happen unexpectedly), but getting a stale bill can be worse. Sending bills out on time is professional, it's a good check on yourself to make sure that you're regularly communicating with your client. It confirms to the client that you value your own work and time, and in many instances makes it easier for the client to actually pay the bill - particularly if the client is a big business (getting stale bills processed in a corporate environment can be a challenge indeed).

BREAKING UP - A CLIENT'S PERSPECTIVE

Clowns to the left of me
Jokers to the right, here I am
Stuck in the middle with you...

Thankfully law firm departures don't resemble the action in Reservoir Dogs, the ridiculously violent (and terrific) movie from which that lyric was borrowed, but they're not always smooth either. Especially when lawyers leave with the intent to carry on their existing practice elsewhere.

In the face of all the tricky separation issues, the client's interests need to be at the forefront. While the idea of categorizing clients as "assets" in a "book of business" may be easy for most lawyers to intellectually compartmentalize, it can be a very uncomfortable and unsettling one from the client's perspective.

Recently, I hired a firm of licensed professionals. Not a law firm, but educated, licensed professionals. I had no pre-existing relationship with either the firm or the professional to whom I was assigned.   I'll call the firm "Failco" and my contact professional "Shirley" (As in, surely you can't be serious).

Everything was going along fine with Shirley.   Then I got a call one evening on my personal cell around 8:45pm, and things got weird.

The voice on the other end was from Fern Failco, the self-proclaimed caretaker of the "Failco" firm name. Her pace was quick and nervous, having the same "just get it over with" kind of speed that I'd use when, say, I needed to tell my Dad that I just airmailed a Mylec Street Hockey Ball through the garage door window. The call went something like this:

"Michael? This is Fern Failco from Failco and I'm sorry to call so late, but I have some very important information I need to tell you. Shirley is no longer with our firm. I needed to call you *immediately* to assure you that you will continue to receive the highest level of professional service from us. I'm going to assign Bob to your account. He'll call you tomorrow, but I want you to know this firm has my family's name on it, and I am committed to making sure your account is handled professionally. Our experience and professionalism is of utmost importance to us."

Her overuse (actually, misuse) of the word "professional" conveyed to me the same sincerity level as Antony's "honorable man" praise of Brutus speech in Julius Caesar.

She offered no explanation, invited no questions, gave no options. She gave no insight at all on why this was urgent information - *to me*. I'd never even spoken with Fern before.

"Slow down Fern. I like your firm, but I also like Shirley. I hear what you've told me, but obviously I have questions and I'm sure you'll understand that I'll want to speak with Shirley myself."

At that point, Fern's nervousness turned ever-so-slightly into defensiveness, and she started leaning on me a bit. I was ready for her to jump right to the, "Your engagement is with US, and you're OURS," *within 10 minutes of speaking with me for the first time*, but she had the sense to stop short of that.

I don't ever think I felt more like a fungible line item on someone's Excel spreadsheet than I did after I hung up with her; that is, until I spoke with Shirley the next day.

Much to Fern's chagrin, the next morning I called Shirley. Not surprisingly, it sounded like the whole hoo-hah was over some business issue between Shirley and Fern that ultimately resulted in Shirley getting canned. Shirley claimed she had no idea this was going to happen, which didn't seem very credible to me either. After giving me "her side" she encouraged me to write a letter to a state regulatory department *demanding that I be "released to her"* (her words), because - I kid you not - "*That's what my lawyer told me to tell you.*" Lawyers now? How comforting!

Having witnessed similar shenanigans as a young law firm associate, at least I wasn't totally naive to what was actually happening. However, I couldn't imagine how others would've felt in that situation, people who aren't really that familiar with these kind of business disputes. I thought about my kid sister (a Special Ed teacher) getting that series of calls, or my folks.

In the end, Fern and Sally both failed, but the experience is a great example on how the client's interests need to be paramount. In many cases, the client's choice between sticking with a firm or going with the departing professional is easy and clear, but that isn't always true, and in those cases it's especially important to be sensitive to the position the client is getting placed into.

Complying with ethical rules and formal requirements is obviously essential, but only to a bare minimum.   A client should never be pressured, thrown in the middle of a business dispute, or made to feel like part of a "book of business" - a fungible asset in a disputed portfolio.

Keeping the focus squarely on the *client's* interests is the first step in ensuring a smooth and truly professional handling of a breakup.

LEGAL PRACTICE MANAGEMENT ADVICE FROM YESTERYEAR

Over the Thanksgiving weekend I spent some time cleaning out the closet in my home office. Thankfully I don't have a ton of papers to get rid of, but I still have quite the archive of old files and data, stored on everything from Zip disks to 3.5inch floppies (!). (Note: A lot of my important stuff is, of course, backed up in the cloud).

Mixed among my old copies of FPS: Football and Diablo, I came across a few notes on advice I was given during my time as a young lawyer. Stuff I used to jot down, specifically with the intention of someday looking back upon it. Now, with more than a few years of work under my belt, it was fun to see how some of these gems held up (or not) over time. Here's a few to start - 2 not-so-good, 2 really good.

Not-So-Good Advice

Setting: 1994, my first day of work at my firm. I walked into my über-cool new "real lawyer" office, with my (awesome) nameplate on the wall, looked at my desk and asked "Where's my computer?"

Not-So-Good Advice #1: "Lawyers don't use computers – we don't get paid to type."

Yikes. Not very Nostradamus-like there. By 1994, I'd already been a computer geek for several years (all the way back to writing BASIC games on my TRS-80 and beloved Apple IIe), and was already good with WordPerfect and Lotus 1-2-3.

I could type as fast as I could speak and - more importantly - had become accustomed to composing documents on a screen in front of me, on the fly. The general reluctance to embrace new technology - certainly far from unique to my own firm - was something I got to experience for several years after that, lasting until I started working with technology companies.

Better advice: be open minded on new technology, consider the trends, try to stay ahead of the curve - or at least try to understand where things are heading.

Setting: One year in with my firm, 1995, hanging out with a few paralegals and secretaries in the lunchroom.

Not-So-Good Advice #2: "We're all on the same team, but be careful mixing too much with staff."

If what the partner meant to say was "be careful to remember to always preserve client confidentialities", or something along those lines, it would've jumped into the "good" column - and certainly wouldn't have been limited to staff interactions. The truth was, as a young lawyer, there were many occasions when if it weren't for good staff relationships, I'd have been completely sunk. Like many others, I had the academic creds. - top grades, Law Review, MBA, etc. - but experienced admins and paralegals had the kind of real-life, practical knowledge that only actual time in the field provides.

These folks always know plenty of extremely useful things - such as knowing which corporate service company to use when you need something filed at 4:00 p.m. on Friday, knowing the exact way an overly picky partner or client wants a draft marked up, or knowing the best way to get a massive mailing out the door at the last minute (and it's always at the last minute).

Better advice: Spend time getting to know, and learning from, experienced staff.

Great Advice

Great Advice #1: Keep Your Client Informed and Up-To-Speed.

This one might be self-evident to a lot of folks, but it wasn't to me coming right out of school. Whether you're working as an associate at a larger firm and your "client" is a senior partner, or if you're thrown right into the fire and working directly with actual clients, you need to communicate early and often. Make sure you're clear with your client on the objectives, scope, and strategy of a project. You need to make sure that whatever you're working on, whatever you're billing for, the client is kept up to speed.

Consider (or ask your partner to consider) if the client ought get a copy of that research memo you drafted, or of the correspondence you sent to opposing counsel - no matter how inconsequential it may seem to you at the time. Communicate, communicate, communicate. Working at a larger firm can sometimes create an academic or distant feel, but never let yourself forget that real money, and real people with real problems are at stake. Make sure the client knows what's going on.

Great Advice #2: Send Your Bills On Time.

As a young lawyer, you can get the perception that nobody likes to get a bill - and that perception can end up justifying billing procrastination. However, let me tell you what's worse -

far worse: Getting a big surprise bill that's far more than you expect, and several months after the work was performed.

As a consumer of legal services, I can assure you that there is nothing worse (and no more certain way of me looking for a dramatic discount) than to stall on sending me a bill. Typically, as a business consumer, I'm used to paying my vendor bills on a regular schedule, and usually pretty darn close to when the services for which I'm paying were performed. When that doesn't happen, it creates all sorts of problems for me. First, I need to try and go back and remember what actually happened, reconstruct my own records, and so forth. Second, if I'm not the final sign off person on payment myself, you can be sure I'm going to have to explain all the facts to that final sign off person, and then paying the bill becomes a "process" rather than a routine event.

You don't want to land in the "out of the ordinary" pile when you're looking to get paid. In a way, this is all a repeat of the first piece of advice: communicate. If you're communicating properly, the client should never be completely surprised by the amount of a current, timely bill. Plus, a timely bill - one that's consistent with communicated expectations - is far more likely to be paid quickly, and without substantial haggling.

Now that's great advice.

HOW LEGAL PROJECT MANAGEMENT REMOVES BARRIERS TO NEW BUSINESS FROM ENTREPRENEURS

I recently spoke with a good friend of mine, an experienced entrepreneur who has raised capital, launched innovative technologies, and built up several teams. He's also a consumer of legal services.

A technology/market "visionary" type, he often tries to keep his focus primarily on those specific aspects of his ventures, and has his team take direct responsibility for managing other things such as lawyers, accountants, and so forth. However, in this case several of his key "go to" folks were tied up in other projects - so he flew solo on a lot of these things, including working with a "BigLaw" firm on some operational matters.

(Note: As an aside, one of the major benefits of entrepreneurial success – whether it's in the context of launching a tech venture or a new law firm – is identifying great team members and keeping them. Finding bodies to fill job descriptions is usually pretty easy. Finding smart, loyal, experienced people who have the personality and skill to thrive in a fast-paced, rapidly changing environment can be ridiculously difficult – whether your new venture has plenty of cash or not).

The "BigLaw" Example

My friend relayed his "BigLaw" experience to me and it highlighted what is, I believe, something of a paradox in the legal services business. A paradox that relates to some of the LPM ideas we've been kicking around. I'll explain:

When he first engaged this particular "BigLaw" firm, he didn't really need access to hundreds of super smart lawyers to mull over complex transactional issues, or the threat of an army of litigators. However, the suggestion of insider/preferred access to prime venture capital firms was alluring at a time when capital markets for startups was bone dry. That access never really materialized, but the firm became the default firm for routine transactional stuff.

We were talking through some nits involving a potential investment, and I suggested that we rope in one of his lawyers for some added advice.

"Good idea", he says, "But it'll cost us over $600/hour." Yikes!

Then he fills me in on the rest. "A few months back I sent them up our terms of service to look through. They assigned me to another attorney for that. When I reviewed the work and noticed a few things I thought needed to be covered and weren't, he told me that this wasn't really his area of expertise and should pass it on to another attorney at the firm – and I was billed thousands for it."

Now the paradox: at a time when many firms are working harder than ever to generate and maintain business, here is a guy who has (and should continue) to generate tons of interesting, profitable legal work, but he is being discouraged to do so solely by the cost and uncertainty and other inefficiencies associated with obtaining it.

He values the good legal advice, he knows where to ask for it, and he is happy to pay for it. However, the high cost and uncertainty involved in the delivery of the service has deterred him from engaging it. That's a lost opportunity for both parties.

Embracing LPM

Entrepreneur complaints about lawyer practices have been well addressed before. For example,"Top 10 Reasons Why Entrepreneurs Hate Laywers" is a great piece written by Scott Edward Walker of The Walker Corporate Law Group. The title may be a bit much - it may be a bit more accurate to say that it's the practices the entrepreneurs take issue with, not the value of good legal advice itself. Nevertheless, many of the concerns are valid.

The tie-in to Legal Productivity Management (LPM) is evident. Though not necessarily a primary driver, it's easy to imagine how some of the project management techniques we discuss in *Legal Productivity, the book*, would have impacted my friend's decision to buy some additional legal advice as opposed to forego it.

Embracing LPM techniques early on in a relationship can not only help streamline servicing the particular matter at issue, but also promote and encourage additional work in the future.

Dramatically reducing the amount of cost and "process uncertainty" associated with legal work can go a long way toward removing the obstacles otherwise holding back new business.

Must-Haves for Law Firms: IOLTA and Branded Email

Originally published on Rocket Matter's Legal Productivity blog by guest blogger Brian Lewis (http://www.brianjosephlewis.com). Mr. Lewis is an attorney and journalist, currently practicing in Mid-Missouri. He holds a J.D. from NYU School of Law and a B.A. from Yale.

Sine Qua Non – If you're a BattleStar Galactica fan, you know how this concept of, 'that without which', can be a romantic ideal.

If you're a lawyer, however, you're probably more familiar with it being the worst sort of detail: the wanted nail that cost the battle.

This post deals two Sine Qua Nons for lawyers in solo and small practice face every day: the Lawyer Trust Account and a branded email account.

Lawyer Trust Account

Most states have adopted an IOLTA best practice guideline for small practitioners. To put it simply, I'll quote from the California Bar, as their description of an IOLTA account puts it best:

"Lawyers who handle small amounts of money for their clients, or money that is held for a short period of time, must participate in the program by depositing these funds into an Interest on Lawyers' Trust Account (IOLTA). (When lawyers hold funds from one client that are large enough or held for a long enough period to earn interest for that client, the funds are segregated so that the client receives the interest)."

That baseline flexibility of an IOLTA, where big deposits are segregated so as not to unjustly enrich and simultaneously deprive clients by virtue of their money residing in the same account, is the solution to the problem of commingled funds.

The problem of commingling funds is so prevalent that it dominates much of today's regulation of lawyers.

So, there's really no controversy here: you need to get an IOLTA set up to catch pre-paid fees and hold them for draw down as they're earned. That includes modern 'retainers', which are essentially pre-paid legal fees. True retainers aren't earned against and may go directly into earned fees accounts.

Branded Email Accounts

While there's no statute requiring a branded email account, I believe there should be. It's just like, or even more so, the ideal heir of the lawyer's stationery and letterhead. Very much like many malpractice insurance agencies will require you to update them every time you change letterhead, a forward thinking agency should also require you to update them when you create a branded email account. This is for your own protection quite honestly, as you wouldn't want to have to provide access to every email you write from your personal account, nor would you want to have to operate from moarlegal4u@gmail.com forever.

Google has a wonderful Google apps project that allows you to go ahead and make use of that URL from Go Daddy that you squatted a while back just to save until you learned how to use cold fusion and really make an awesome site. Now, you can start getting email at you@[yoururl].com instead of actually having to make a site first.

It's quite simple, just go to google.com. Search for google apps. Click on custom Gmail, and follow the directions. It took a little bit of familiarity with Go Daddy to make it work for me. But I'm now findable at brian@brianlewislaw.com. Email me if you get it working!

5 Bad Habits Of Business Lawyers

First of all, business lawyers rock. They're among the sharpest thinking professionals in business, routinely pulling together complex deal structures, making sense out of rules and regulations, and giving great general business advice to clients. (Disclosure: Yes I'm biased, I started my career as a business lawyer.)

Since leaving law for the tech world I've been on the client side, a consumer of primarily corporate and transactional legal services. During those 10+ years, I've worked with several different business lawyers, running the gamut from savvy solos to Big Law partners, and they've almost all been outstanding. In the rare instances when my experience hasn't been a great one, it's usually been attributed to one of five things:

1. Redonkulous Billing Practices

If you send a bill for the "XYZ contract negotiation" more than a month or so after the XYZ deal closed, you're creating at least 2 problems for me. I know you don't mean to create trouble - in fact, you might even think you're doing me a favor by holding off on the bill, but you're not.

First, if it's a significant size bill, it probably means I'm going to have to spend time re-analyzing things that are - by now - a likely distant memories to me (Yuck! more admin "make work"). Stale invoices have a good chance of going to the bottom of the to-do pile, along with the other things I'm putting off until I have more time to look into them. It's not a great pile to be in if you're looking for quick turnaround.

Second, if I'm in a spot where I can't personally authorized the final sign-off on the bill, I'm going to have to explain to someone else why I'm turning in a late bill. The people who actually pay bills - the accounting folks (I'm also one of those), really dig things that are "normal", "routine", "ordinary course" – you get the idea. Things that are easy to process, simple to record. On the other hand, things that fall outside of the norm, raise eyebrows and at best, end up resulting in extra scrutiny. Translation: delay.

So, to get paid faster, please send me the bill on time. Neither of us are better off if you stall.

That said, if you're having trouble getting your bills out on time, consider investing in a simple practice management app. Bottom line: It'll save you a ton of time. I promise you'll quickly recover the $2/day.

2. Not Really Understanding My Business

If I'm talking about our "key metrics" and you're on the other end of the line furiously Googling for inches-to-centimeter formulas, trouble probably isn't far off. That's a silly exaggeration, but you get the point.

So many business attorneys have such an incredibly valuable accumulation of knowledge to share. You have seen hundreds of deals and been part of negotiations that ranged from silky smooth and amicable to crazy contentious and difficult. I get giddy thinking about having access to all that experience. However, without some specific knowledge of what drives my particular industry (or better yet, my specific business), it's just not nearly as valuable as it could be.

Ideally, it would be great if you could invest a little time now and then to read up on what's happening in my area, read our press releases once in a while, ask me for a copy of our financials, or even just meet for coffee to chat about what we're working on lately. If you have the level of knowledge of our business equal to that of, say - someone on our advisory board - your ability to help increases exponentially.

The client has responsibility here too. On my end, I should never ask you to help me with a project until I invest the time to thoroughly explain the entire big picture: why we're doing something, what our goals are, any "politics" or sensitivities involved, any trapdoors or land mines I can think of, and so forth. It's my responsibility to get you all the information, as opposed to just dumping something onto you and expecting miracles. (I was on the bad end of that a few times early in my career; I know it's the worst.)

An experienced business lawyer who knows my business well enough to be able to accurately and proactively advise - to help me avert potential problems or seize opportunities before they actually emerge – that is an incredible and valuable partner.

3. Wasting Time On (Likely) Trivial Issues Or, Worse Yet, Spending Time On Trivial Issues While Missing Important Ones.

It's tough to hear how my lawyer has tried to mark up the indemnity clause three times already yet "the other side" (usually more accurately characterized as "my business partner to be") is being unreasonable and won't budge. This is a double bummer when I'm independently reviewing the same document and notice that the payment terms, or some other material business term, doesn't remotely resemble the term sheet or what we had discussed in the meeting.

Yes, I know the "boilerplate" can be important, and I absolutely want you to point things out to me that you find grossly unreasonable or uncustomary. However, if it's something that could be a teensy bit more favorable if we drafted it differently, or something that could protect us a little better in the 1 time out of 1,000,000 that the event may occur. That's cool too – but let's save that stuff until we're happy with the key business terms. That works both ways; that is, if I'm the one (unintentionally) focusing on minutiae, please tell me in no uncertain terms. In buying legal services, I'm acutely aware that the customer is NOT always right.

Basically, if we're doing this right, neither one of us should ever have to ask the other: "We're holding up this deal over that?"

Also, if you and I are providing the first draft of documents, let's agree to provide a first draft that's fair and mutual instead of trying to make every little bit completely one-sided. That one little move can not only save oodles of time, but can also send a very valuable message.

4. Passing too much work to inexperienced attorneys

Delegating work to junior (read: less expensive) associates can be a good thing. Sometimes, junior associates can handle certain things more efficiently. However, frequently that lower billing rate doesn't offset the additional time it takes for a well-intentioned, hard-working, smart but inexperienced associate to get something done. Basically, try not to send a bill out that includes time or costs that are more fairly charged to your own firm's training budget.

Actually, I think this is going to become an increasingly tricky issue for the entire profession as technology (e.g. document assembly) evolves. What used to be "junior associate" work can now frequently either be done by the client (with a senior lawyer "proofing" it later on), or directly by a senior lawyer in an extremely short amount of time. This puts a squeeze on the junior transactional lawyer, and that can mean less of an opportunity to learn the ropes.

I think all lawyers have an obligation to help train the next generation, and that clients (particularly in-house attorneys and law departments) need to become even more accepting, even encouraging of junior corporate attorneys observing, attending meetings and deal negotiations, and so forth. However, the expense of the junior's time – at least insofar as hourly billing goes - should usually be borne solely by the firm. It's an interesting and important issue and a topic for further discussion in a separate piece.

5. Inventing Non-Issues, A.K.A. Putting a Turd in the Punchbowl.

A corollary of the "don't get hung up on trivial issues" is the: "Wait, what if ...", followed by a crazy, convoluted fact pattern akin to the one offered up by your Criminal Law professor on your 1L final exam. This is particularly gnarly when offered up about 15 minutes after we've finally reached agreement on what everyone believes to be the last key business issue. Yes, it's useful to be able to carefully identify the single fact pattern that lies 214 legs down the decision tree, that if materialized, could result in a consequence that neither I nor my new business partner would anticipate.

At the same time, there are few worse feelings in a business context than everyone feeling as though they've finally successfully struck a deal, only for the lawyers to start raising brand new issues that: (a) for whatever reason they hadn't thought of during the negotiation; and (b) are theoretically possible, but in practical terms extremely unlikely to occur.

In the rare event when there's a good reason for that (e.g. the facts suddenly, dramatically changed), we can "off-line" it; that is, have a private side conference to talk it through. The way NOT to raise it is in the very common situation where all parties are on a conference call, none of us are in the same physical locations, and we're all about to give the final OKs to sign. The dreaded "what if …." gets thrown out onto the Skype line like a deal grenade, and then there's five seconds of dead silence until it explodes into a bunch of mumbling and "let's reconvene". If there are big issues, let's try to surface them early and – if they unavoidably come up late – make sure they're really important enough to make all of us dump out that big tasty bowl of punch we're just about to drink.

As I mentioned, business lawyers are among the smartest and hard-working in the profession. Avoiding a few of these things can make the relationship with a business even more valuable and mutually beneficial.

LEARNING THE BIZ LAWYER ROPES - 21ST CENTURY STYLE

When I first started my career, I was a young business lawyer at a great firm in WNY. I had just graduated from school, and was fortunate enough to have received an offer from the firm where I worked as a summer associate. (Sadly, I'm told that the clerk-to-associate path is no longer the fairly clear route that it once was.)

I loved law school and business school. Like a lot of my peers at the time, I did the JD/MBA "two-fer" and take a little pride in saying I was good at it - at least insofar as good is measured by honors, grades and whatnot. That experience translated into feeling fairly well-trained, reasonably educated, and moderately confident to embark on my career.

Learning in the Real World (Then)

That said, it probably took all of 15 minutes "in practice" to discover the cavernous difference between succeeding in school and being a good professional. Back then (early '90s), being a junior associate in a corporate department meant cutting one's teeth on incorporations, basic closing documents, fairly "standard" contracts, and periodically getting a chance to sit down with one of the senior partners and take notes on a conference call. Luckily, I had very patient, experienced and ridiculously smart partners - and an amazing support team - to work for and learn from. (Thanks to: Chris, Bob, Greg, Gust, Anthony, Bill, Dan, Ken, Priscilla, Kelly, Barb, and many others.) I got the chance to pick up on how Chris resolved a tricky deal point, or how Bob could cleverly draft a lease provision in a way that made both sides happy. Learning by "supervised doing"; learning by watching how it's done.

That's primarily how my class learned, how we became experienced. After a few years, I assembled my own customized "form book" (comprised then of a 3-ring binder with photocopied samples), and started working on more advanced things. Being a lifelong techie, this was right about the time when I was starting to store everything on disks while I ran up ridiculous bills chatting on AOL and sending e-mails. Soon thereafter, I was off to work in the technology business, taking a seat on the other side of the attorney-client relationship. Little did I know that I might've been one of the last of the dinosaurs, in the sense of being trained in the classic "junior associate" way.

Learning in the Real World (Now)

Now, as Richard Susskind and others have pointed out, technology is rapidly making all these "teeth cutting" opportunities completely obsolete. Young lawyers face an extremely tough labor market as it is, many are either forced to immediately hang out a shingle (sooner than most might want) or work in a firm environment where they're often expected to be able to hit the ground running at full speed. Clients aren't accepting even a hint of "training" priced into their bill, and work once handled almost exclusively by outside junior lawyers is now often managed completely in-house.

In the face of rapidly emerging disruptive technology, where does a young transactional lawyer get the critical practical experience necessary to become a really good "deal person"?

The issue was recently addressed in "Law 2.0: Intelligent Architecture For Transactional Law", an event that was part of the Silicon Flatirons Roundtable Series on Entrepreneurship, Innovation and Public Policy.

Recognizing that clients want "value-adding" lawyers, and that it takes skills and judgment to deliver such services, several suggestions were offered. One that I thought sounded particularly interesting was a "Moot Court" for deal work. Another cool idea was a multiplayer video game, like a "Second Life" for legal issues. Certainly, clinics and seminar-level courses at law schools can also be instructive, but nothing replaces the experience one gains from helping clients work through real problems and help them close real deals.

The Future of Legal Learning & Technology

As legal technology continues to evolve – from document assembly to project management to embedded legal knowledge (e.g. documents that are physically designed to automatically prevent non-compliance) – alternative methods of training must evolve as well. Will larger firms simply choose to absorb the costs of training, potentially using gains realized by technology to offset those additional costs? How will all of this impact upon the general quality of legal services available 10, 20 years out, if at all?

I suspect that ultimately this presents another exciting opportunity for law schools, practicing lawyers, and technology providers to proactively work more closely together, designing and testing new technology-driven training solutions, as opposed to what has arguably been a general pattern of technology independently charging forward, and then encouraging adoption.

OFFICE SPACE (A FOUR-PART SERIES)

PART I: FINDING A HOME FOR YOUR LAW FIRM

> **Dom Portwood:** Hi, Peter. What's happening? We need to talk about your TPS reports.
>
> **Peter Gibbons:** Yeah. The cover sheet. I know, I know. Uh, Bill talked to me about it.

Whoops .... wrong "Office Space"

Option 1: Leasing a traditional office (or offices) on your own – if you can afford it.

Prior to listing out some actual tips on leasing physical office space, take a step back and approach with caution even if - and particularly when - it feels as though the work is piling up and clients are pouring in.

For any small business - law firm included - recurring rent can end up being one of the biggest operating expenses after payroll, and also one of the most difficult to defer. Like a houseguest that stays too long, once it's signed that lease is always there, and the payment seems as though it'll never leave.

Also, unlike a lot of trade creditors who will often give you a break when payment is late by a few days, landlords (particularly those with steep mortgages), usually don't respond too favorably to blown 10-day grace periods.

Given that, if you've chosen to make a leased office your true home base or storefront, know that your landlord can inadvertently become a pretty powerful influence on the business side of your firm.

A quick aside and cautionary tale...

Early in my career I had the opportunity to work on several high profile Chapter 11 bankruptcy cases involving retail, storefront businesses. As a young lawyer, in between plodding through the oh-so-fun bankruptcy schedules (they never showed THAT work on "LA Law"), I was lucky enough to also spend some time with senior business executives learning how these businesses got into the spot they were in.

Many shared the same pattern. Each started small, rapidly grew sales - some achieving crazy initial success - and they aggressively expanded at a pace that matched their quick sales growth. For these retail businesses, that meant quickly adding stores, which in turn meant adding several real property leases to their operating costs.

When the business growth rate inevitably leveled off, they were stuck in a highly leveraged position with big lease payments due each month. Strapped for liquidity and unable to keep up with all the fixed monthly rent payments, understandably, the last straw was that landlords started taking action.

Nothing highlights better how an otherwise decent core business can be seriously and immediately jeopardized by a landlord than hearing the utter panic in a client's voice when (prior to bankruptcy) they've been unexpectedly locked out! The effect of that kind of action can quickly snowball throughout an organization, and pretty soon those landlords become the tail wagging the dog.

The analogy between a retail chain and a law firm certainly isn't perfect, but some of the lessons can definitely overlap. Be conscious of the leverage on your business that you're creating by signing a traditional term lease.

There are often situations where from a business perspective, taking on additional financial risk can be justifiable - for example, investments in networking or marketing. However, barring some clear, strategic upside that directly supports one of those objectives (such as leasing space that is assured to generate new business or referrals just by virtue of its location) - "conservative" is a good way to lean when leasing physical space.

If you're not certain you can comfortably afford that space, especially during times when business or cash flow may be temporarily slow, you're likely better off looking at options other than leasing physical space on your own. You don't need that extra pressure.

PART II: LEASING TRADITIONAL SPACE

Here we will discuss 3 key factors to consider when you're ready to lease space on your own:

1. Scope Out a Good Location

When leasing space on your own, location is paramount. It has a direct impact on your schedule, your personal life, your existing clients and potentially your ability to attract more clients.   For example, litigators may find that an office close to the courthouse can both save huge amounts of time (which can translate into thousands of dollars of opportunity cost) and provide for all kinds of terrific business development opportunities.   Being close to the place where your colleagues are routinely gathering can make it extremely convenient to do some old-school social networking. Having a home close to the action can also dramatically improve your own quality of life. Similarly, attorneys with a business focus might consider laying down some roots where accountants and financial planners roam.

Specifics vary, but the general point holds across the board: don't underestimate location.

2. Pay Attention To Details

This concept will be obvious and oversimplified to an attorney experienced with real property leases, but to others not so much.   For folks new to leasing there can sometimes be a tendency to focus only on the perceived "big" points like price per square foot and term. However, there are a lot of other things that one needs to understand, negotiate, or consciously choose to not negotiate. Sometimes these terms are covered in the lease (which is usually provided by the landlord), but sometimes they're not. It's not just what's in the lease that's important, what isn't there can be equally so. Here are just a few practical things to think about on that point:

Improvements:

Depending on how long your term is, the landlords may agree to make some improvements at their expense: new carpet and new paint are fairly common examples.   Even if the landlord won't pay for it, you need to understand what you are allowed to do on your own, what requires consent, and so forth. Don't just assume consent will be automatic.

Unique Financial Terms:

Many landlords will request that you personally guarantee the lease. The existence, duration, and scope of these guarantees can often be negotiated. For instance, a personal guarantee may only be required for a portion of the lease term, or it may be limited to rent payments alone (as opposed to other tenant obligations).   Make sure you're absolutely clear on it. Similarly, make certain you clarify who is responsible for what with respect to the heat, A/C, and other structural issues - sometimes the tenant is responsible for minor repairs, filter upkeep, and so forth.   Also, in many markets it's now fairly customary for landlords to offer some "free rent" as an incentive to attract new tenants. Free rent usually comes with longer term commitments (3+ years or more), but the economics of each particular market is unique - it can't hurt to ask.

Important Logistics:

Is parking an issue? Do you need to make sure you have a minimum number of spaces available during business hours? Does the space meet your needs with respect to electric, internet, phones, etc.? (Many of these individual items we'll hit in more detail in subsequent posts). What about signage? Weekend/off-hours access? Security?Before you sign the lease, make certain you also do a walk-through and thoroughly inspect the property before your payment obligation starts.

3. Appearance Counts

It's important that your office accurately portrays you, your personality and your practice, particularly if it's a place where you will be frequently meeting with clients and colleagues.   Make sure you include a budget for a modest amount of decorative and other miscellaneous work in your financial evaluation of the lease. It's unlikely that the office will come in complete "practice ready" shape.

These days, the image of an opulent, luxurious office with huge conference rooms filled with $2,000 designer chairs isn't necessarily the message of "powerful" and "successful" that it once was; rather, today it can easily communicate an impression of "out of touch." That's good news, because having that type of a pricey set up just isn't necessary anymore. On the other hand, that's not carte blanche to place zero value on appearance.   It's not going to inspire confidence in anyone to walk into their lawyer's office and see stuff that's old, mismatched, ratty, or uncomfortable.   It's also not going to be good for you, considering you may be spending an awful lot of time there.

There's a massive gap between the extremes, a lot of room in the middle.

First, nice quality, stylish office furniture can be found inexpensively in all sorts of places these days. From office liquidation stores to consignment shops to Craigslist, there are plenty of options available, even on a shoestring budget.

Next, get rid of clutter - particularly excess paper. Don't have lots of paper lying around. It's messy and it subtly conveys all kinds of wrong messages from "I'm completely disorganized" to "I'm really too busy for you." Invest in a scanner and get all that paper scanned, organized, <u>made web-accessible, secure, and regularly backed up in the cloud</u>. Having paper all over the place is unnecessary, psychologically bad, and unreliable.

Lastly, be sensitive to the clients you're serving. Leave the boring, generic office prints (the art equivalent to <u>Muzac</u>) in the garage. Instead, consider who your visitors are and what might be most visually appealing to them - and don't forget a nicely framed diploma and license are always appropriate - most folks like to see your credentials.

Make your space personal, professional, organized, and welcoming to your visitors. It's not an expensive endeavor, but it does take some budget and some thought, and it's worth it.

Part III: Sharing

If <u>leasing space on your own</u> isn't quite optimal or financially desirable, sharing space with another lawyer can be another option to consider.

Sharing space has the obvious upside of reducing cost, sometimes enabling you to be in a location that you couldn't otherwise (comfortably) afford on your own. However, sharing space with another lawyer can also provide a solo or small firm with valuable direct access to other professionals. That kind of "right there" access to a colleague can be terrific when you're looking for a common sense check on a pleading, a drafting idea for a contract, or some specialized knowledge or insight on a complex matter.

Similarly, your own insight is likely to be asked for as well and ultimately, that kind of interaction can directly lead to some quality referrals.

Considerations for Sharing

1. Compatibility

Obviously you want to avoid sharing space with a lawyer you don't like or respect, or has any reputation issues that can unfairly impact on your practice.   If you don't know the lawyer personally, do your diligence.

Remember too, it's not just the lawyer you're concerned about in the compatibility analysis. His or her clients matter as well.   The lawyer may be a terrific person to share an office with, but the clients may not be the type that mix well with your own practice. A real estate lawyer who spends the majority of time meeting with clients at the County Clerk's office, presents an entirely different set of office sharing circumstances than a consumer bankruptcy attorney who may been meeting with multiple clients constantly walking in and out of the office, taking up parking spots, and the like.

2. Watch For Conflicts; Protect Confidentiality

Before entering into a sharing relationship, check for conflicts.   If there are potential conflicts between lawyers, your respective fundamental practice areas, or your respective clients - or such conflicts seem likely to arise in the future - it can be a flashing yellow warning light.

Also, sharing office space triggers extra caution with respect to client confidentiality concerns. If you retain a lot of papers (which you shouldn't need to do anyway), take care to avoid leaving confidential papers where others can see. Hitting "print", then taking a phone call and forgetting that confidential document sitting on the printer is not going to work in a shared workspace environment.

Actually, sharing space can also serve as another catalyst to migrate away from messy, disorganized "old school" paper pushing. Instead, get that paper scanned and uploaded to a secure, web-accessible cloud application that continually backs up your data. For a lot of lawyers, migrating to the cloud will immediately improve productivity, security and continuity.

3. Clarification of Status

Sharing an office does not create a partnership, but everyone should take care to make sure the public isn't confused. Make sure that things like the office signage and your letterhead unambiguously communicate that you are individual lawyers independently providing service. If you have staff, remind your staff to be sensitive with respect to this potential confusion. Clients need to be clear that the office sharing arrangement is just that.

Finally, regardless of what you've agreed to split or share, NEVER share or commingle client trust accounts. **Ever.**

4. Write It Up

Similar to the point about "Pay Attention To Details" in Part II, don't overlook the need to document your relationship. Whether it takes the form of a formal sublease or some other document (which may also require advance permission or consent from the landlord or owner of the property), it's important to spell out the terms of the sharing relationship. At a minimum, you want to make sure how and what office resources are to be shared, how and when payments will be made, how parking spaces are allocated (if parking is tight), and how any conference rooms or meeting areas will be split.

In the next and last part of this series we'll take a look at the virtual office, primarily from the standpoint of working from home.

PART IV: THE HOME/VIRTUAL OFFICE

The last option in this Office Space series is the virtual office. The virtual office can be defined in a myriad of ways, but one of the most common iterations is simply working out of your home. Aside from the obvious cost savings (and potential tax benefit), there are several Pros and Cons to consider:

Pros to the Home/Virtual Office

No Office "Roomies"

In other words, barring client visits, you're free to dress casually, listen to music at whatever volume you'd like, eat at your desk, use your speakerphone, burn candles, and otherwise create a work environment that is tailored solely and exclusively to *Numero Uno*.

No Commute

Depending upon where you live, working at home can easily add several minutes up to a few hours of productivity a day. Similarly, you may actually live *closer* to the places you need to periodically be (court, county clerk's office, client offices, *etc.*) and thus, could be significantly cutting your out-of-pocket commuting costs.

Cons to the Home/Virtual Office

Interruptions

When working at home, spouses, significant others and/or kids need to respect the home/office distinction. Realistically, the adults in the picture either inherently have the ability to respect this or they don't - and you probably know whether they do already. If they don't, contending with that can be very difficult, and end up affecting both your professional and personal life.

Self-Discipline

For your part, you need to respect that you can't be "on the clock" 24/7. In some ways, working from home can be a big enabler for workaholics because the work is always right there, staring back at you. As lawyers know, setting bright-line rules is usually not a successful approach. However, barring the occasional real client emergency, it is generally possible to set down some general parameters and try to keep business to business hours.

Perception issues

Some clients will not necessarily look favorably upon lawyers working out of their homes, but that perception is changing fast as technology continues to evolve (the huge, opulent "traditional" office also has its own, sometimes worse, set of perception problems). In addition, for certain projects like discovery production, due diligence, deal closings, board meetings, *etc.*, it's possible - and even preferable - to work with the client right at the client's office.

Zoning Or Use Restrictions

That cranky neighbor, or the self-proclaimed King of your Condo Association, will undoubtedly get all bent out of shape if he sees clients periodically coming and going from your home. Be aware that if your property isn't in an area zoned for your practice, you could end up spending a lot of time you didn't plan for doing a bunch of extra favors or seeking variances.

Networking

When working at home, it's easy to get pigeonholed. While social media certainly makes this less of an issue than it once was, "old school" networking is something that can require some additional conscious effort when you're at home. It's important to do all the networking activities (lunches, lectures, schmoozing, etc.) that you'd otherwise be doing if you were working out of a "traditional" office.

Purchasing the necessary equipment. You're most likely to need:

1. A reliable laptop and scanner.

2. A comfortable office-type chair and desk.

3. Web-based practice management software for billing, calendar, contacts, document management and trust accounting.

4. A phone system (virtual receptionists are also available to help with client service and efficiency at reasonable rates).

OVERWHELMED? CONSIDER OUTSOURCING

It's terrific to be busy. That said, sometimes "busy" can very quickly devolve into "swamped." You want to take care of all of your clients while ensuring that each gets the absolute best service possible, yet that clock on the wall reminds you that there are only 24 hours in a day - and you'd like to sleep for at least a few of them. Good news: Outsourcing is a trend that continues to pick up momentum, and it's a practice that's continuing to rapidly evolve and improve.

It's not just for big firms, and it doesn't necessarily mean sending work overseas. Solos and small firms can realize many benefits by outsourcing substantive legal work to qualified, independent, US-based lawyers.

Why Solos and Small Law Firms Should Work With Contract Lawyers and How To Do It

There are a lot of common questions that come up when considering outsourcing, ranging from simple "how-tos" to more complicated ethical considerations. Though more and more solos and small firms are taking advantage of outsourcing opportunities, many others would like a bit more expert insight and guidance before trying it out.

Nationally known speaker Lisa Solomon, Esq. gives an interesting, highly practical, presentation covering what you need to know when you're considering outsourcing. In the presentation (accredited for Florida CLE) - Lisa gives great insight on topics including:

1. The benefits of outsourcing work to a contract lawyer

2. How to find a contract attorney to work with

3. What a good contract lawyer should bring to the table, and

4. Ethical issues in the outsourcing relationship.

So, if you want to learn a little more about outsourcing - and continue to deliver great service to your clients while freeing up a little more of your own time - listen to Lisa's presentation: "Why Solos and Small Law Firms Should Work With Contract Lawyers and How To Do It." It's available anytime, on-demand at RocketCLE.

HOW TO HIRE EFFECTIVELY: UNDERSTANDING YOUR CULTURE

Operating a small business is tough enough. Finding good, reliable people to help you when you're running full-tilt is even tougher.

To the legions of un- and underemployed lawyers out there, it must seem hard to believe that finding help is a challenge. But it's tricky to separate the wheat from the chaff, especially for solo attorneys who are not trained to hire and are juggling a thousand balls at once.

We've examined a number of prescriptive methods for running a business: finding office space, using Facebook for law firm marketing, and many other topics. Now, we're turning our attention to the hiring process.

We'll look at skill assessment and other factors to determine the right person for the bus. Right now, we want to address something many hiring managers overlook that makes all the difference in the world: hiring for culture.

Hiring for Culture

If you haven't worked in a large organization with a defined company culture, this sounds like an abstract, Kumbaya-style concept. But even small firms have their own culture, which is a reflection of the core values of the individuals in the organization's leadership.

When people aren't on the same wavelength and don't gel, it's a lot harder to communicate, stay focused on the same priorities, and work in lock-step. Furthermore, differences in core values can result in low morale, increased stress, and lower productivity in the office.

As Alan Lewis recently wrote in Harvard Business Review, hiring for culture should be priority *numero uno*. Someone with malleable skills can be trained.

Employees who do not adhere to a shared corporate culture dilute it, detracting from the essence that gives your company its identity and helps it achieve aggressive goals. In my view, every organization's hiring process — from Microsoft to PS 90 to everything in between — should screen candidates for the best cultural fit.

So even though a junior associate may have a few years on another candidate, you're probably better off training a new hire that fits your firm's vision rather than someone who doesn't assimilate easily.

That said, skills are hugely important in a knowledge business such as law or software. However, you may be best served in the long run if you side with values, trainability, and less mature skills over someone who has more skills but is less aligned with your way of thinking.

Lewis continues:

Hiring good cultural matches is the best way to assure the continued success of your company. It leads to higher retention (43 percent of our employees have been on board for five or more years), better employee engagement, and deeper connections with customers. Read more of Lewis' article here, including three ways to successfully interview for cultural fit.

HOW TO HIRE EFFECTIVELY PART II: FIRST WHO, THEN WHAT

As the economy slowly heats up, we turn our attention to the hiring process. You can find Part One of this series, <u>How to Hire Effectively for Lawyers : Understanding Your Culture by clicking here</u>.

Have you read <u>*Good to Great*</u>? It's arguably *the* most celebrated business book of the past ten years, and for good reason. Author Jim Collins and his research team painstakingly stitched together real-life data from a handful of successful companies and boiled down common-principles.

First Who, Then What

Chapter Two, "First Who, Then What", is worth the price of the book alone. The whole idea is this: if you get the right people in place in your business, they will be committed to building the best law firm possible. Great companies consider traits such as inherent intelligence, work ethic, and character over specific knowledge or education, which they consider also important but teachable.

Great companies also eschew the notion of having a singular leader drive the vision of the company. The team, not the head honcho establishes the "path to greatness." Most companies rely on a single individual's vision, this works well as long as the leader is around and is making sound decisions. This means that in hiring, you need the A+ candidates, not just those that follow orders.

The Hiring Principles

Finding such talented individuals in this regard is easier said than done, so Collins and his team distilled three hiring principles:

1) When in doubt, keep looking. You may need to hold tight on your growth until you can find the right fit. It's better to hold off on growth than to grow in the wrong way.

2) When you know you need to make a people change, act. And before you fire someone, make sure you just don't have them in the wrong role.

3) Put your best people on your biggest opportunities, not your biggest problems.

Collins' ideas are challenging, and this blog post cannot do justice to the conclusions he and his team came to after years of research. What I find interesting is the recurrence of the idea of hiring people, not first for their skills, but for their inherent abilities. This was reflected in Part One, concerning hiring for culture, and is also echoed in the ideas of Joel Spolsky in his book on hiring, *Smart and Gets Things Done*.

STELLAR BILLING PRACTICES

WHY YOU SHOULD CHARGE HIGHER LEGAL FEES THAN YOUR COMPETITION

How did you establish your legal fees? Whether you bill by the hour, flat fee, or some sort of newfangled alternative fee contraption, you probably got it wrong and to your disadvantage.

If you're like a lot of lawyers, you probably surveyed the local marketplace, came up with a range, and threw a dart at the wall.

Let's take a look at another industry. Jason Fried, who has a big voice in entrepreneurial software circles, recently offered some compelling thoughts on pricing in the recent issue of Inc. Charging too little not only devalues your service, it may compromise your profitability.

The argument goes like this: if you lower your price more people might engage your services. But with more customers, will you be able to effectively service them? Will you need more support staff? Will you become overwhelmed and start missing deadlines? Will you be able to provide the standard of legal counsel that you are happy with?

Jason frames the issue pretty succinctly when discussing the launch of his recent iPad app. Draft:

With a price tag of a buck or two, I think we could have easily sold 10,000 copies of the software. On the surface, that sounds great. But not when you think about all the resources required to serve 10,000 customers.

A good number of those 10,000 people are going to need help. Some are going to complain. Some will request a lot of features. Some will ask a lot of questions... However, our main products sell for $24 to $149 a month. At those prices, we can afford to provide excellent service. Could we provide excellent service for many thousands of additional customers paying a one-time price of $1.99? Would that reduce our ability to service our $24-a-month or $149-a-month customers? We believed it would.

Let's face it: in any group of customers there will be those that are resource drains. And you don't want those customers if they're not paying what's necessary for you to support the whole lot. They shouldn't sink the ship.

Obviously, appropriate pricing for your service is a big topic, exceeding the scope of a blog post. But it starts with data and math. If you're not tracking your hours on flat fee cases, start now. Examine the return of investment on each matter.

That said, tripling your prices at once isn't a good strategy, as software company Zendesk can attest. But people do associate price with quality, so don't be too timid to nudge your prices upwards and above what your competitors charge. You might just be more profitable.

MORE GREAT BILLING ADVICE FOR LAWYERS

Bad billing habits are ultimately one of the key causes of lawyer job dissatisfaction. Failing to send out timely bills (often caused by timesheet procrastination) directly results in higher receivables. Higher receivables lead to higher write-offs. Higher write-offs lead to less revenue. Less revenue leads to all sorts of financial stress - and extra stress is certainly not something lawyers need any more of.

With pressures routinely piling on from court deadlines and increasing client demands, there's just no room for billing problems (which ought to be largely administrative - almost secondary - in nature) to add to the stress burden.

Bill Timely

Lee Rosen over at Divorce Discourse recently posted another terrific testament to the problems associated with letting billing practices slip. In "Are Your Receivables Out of Control", Lee starkly itemizes the real, personal effects of writing down a big bill. He picks a sample write-down amount, applies a typical hourly rate, and reminds us of what that write-down means beyond just the obvious lost revenue.

"[Those] hours [translate] into two or three weeks of extra vacation I could have taken while remaining in the same overall financial position. I could have used that time to float around the Caribbean … or donated that time to charity."

Then the killer: "[I]nstead, I spent that [time] helping someone who decided that I wasn't worth paying." Ouch.

Lee's advice? Confront yourself with what you're really doing when you don't bill timely. Acknowledge that you're essentially electing to grant free financing (even that's assuming you end up being paid in full, which is often not the case). At the same time, he suggests prioritizing the replenishment of your trust balances, getting meaningful retainers in accordance with ethical requirements. Most importantly: ask for the money. Being on the "client" side of the attorney-client relationship myself for so long now, it never ceases to amaze me how many lawyers - unlike most other vendors - rarely send timely bills.   They frequently don't realize that by failing to send a timely bill, it usually makes it more difficult for me to get them quickly paid in full. Stalling on a bill can result in it getting flagged by the client's accounting team as "out-of-the-ordinary", triggering extra levels of scrutiny, and almost always ending up in either delayed payment, a write-down, or both.   A bill sent on time - in more "routine" fashion - can dramatically drive up the prospects for quick, full payment.

Overall, I think the thrust of Lee's message, put bluntly, is: if you're going to do free work, make sure you're doing so on purpose.

Bill As You Work

Respectfully, we'd add to Lee's recommendations a reminder that if time sheets and/or time tracking is contributing to billing challenges in your practice, then try a better option. With today's easy-to-use, reliable, inexpensive options (such as our own "Bill as You Work" technology), time tracking can be relegated to a largely passive task. Not quite completely effortless, but almost - and also far less prone to error.

Improving your billing practices will not only help your revenue stream but can also put a major dent in reducing stress, and increasing overall job satisfaction.

MORE COST CERTAINTY FOR LAW FIRMS = MORE BUSINESS?

The Uncertainty Range

Lack of cost certainty has to be one of the leading reasons why we don't use more legal services. I can't prove it, but I've always suspected there is a heck of a lot of potential legal work out there that doesn't end up on lawyer laptops solely because of the absence of a fixed price (or something close to it.)

Just this weekend an entrepreneur friend – not unlike many other entrepreneur friends– told me he'd really like access to more good legal advice (and trust me, he could use it!) but he's just scared of a bottomless pit of bills. These people are willing to pay for legal services, but they want to know what it's going to cost.

I know that one of the toughest things to hear when discussing a potential engagement is – "Well, this could cost anywhere from $X1 to $X2" with a cavernous gap between the two numbers, and no real analysis of what would drive the difference other than vague references to "what the other side might do", "we don't know what we'll find", and so on.

The "Billable Hour" Situation

The uncertainty range is usually due to the fact that the pricing is premised on billable hours (i.e. the input), when what I'm really interested in is some type of result (i.e. the output). When we buy legal services we're really not looking to buy time, we're looking to buy help to fix a problem, a specific result or a piece of output. Most of the time I could care less if it takes my lawyer eight hours or 80 hours: if the objective is successfully achieved, I'm happy (I also don't think lawyer time is a great proxy for client value, but that discussion deserves its own post).

In a transactional work context, the out-of-pocket cost of the lawyers is often only one small aspect of calculating our expected return associated with a particular project we're involved in. It can be frustrating when virtually all of the other costs associated with, say, an acquisition, can be reasonably estimated but the lawyers find it difficult to estimate their own piece. Lawyers are almost always concerned about how much time they will be investing, when the client is often more concerned with the value to be delivered. The premise that the value delivered is in direct proportion to the hours worked just isn't true.

I can see that there's definitely a lot of situations where a rock-solid "fixed price" arrangement would be tough to work. Complex commercial litigation, involving oodles of discovery, might be just one example. But even in that case, it seems like an experienced commercial litigator should have enough data to know what specific stages of the procedure are likely to cost, based on metrics derived from probably hundreds of prior examples. While it's true that every situation has unique twists and turns, I'd think a lawyer with a significant volume of work under his or her belt should be able to extract some good data from across the entire population of cases – how much lawyer time a certain type of matter tends to take on average, what the external costs are, if any (lien searches, court filings, etc.), what the "costs" are likely to be, and so forth.   So, even if a lawyer wants to count the time as the value being sold, with today's billing technology and practice management software it should be fairly easy to compile individual internal metrics. By doing so, lawyers can offer some better cost certainty to clients while also ensuring that their own financial requirements are met.

The Value In Better Cost Certainty

The incentive in doing so, I'd argue, is a shot at incremental business that wouldn't have otherwise come in absent the ability to offer cost certainty or something close to it. Yes, similar to many other service-based business that have fixed (or close to it) pricing - every individual engagement will not perfectly match estimates. Some will go under, some over. As that happens, and it will, you can pivot as necessary by modifying your terms to reflect actual experiences as new cases and clients are on-boarded.

Also, I don't think this really needs to be absolutely cut-and-dried. It can be phased in. A forward-thinking client might be very willing (eager?) to try a modified approach, where there is some cost certainty – coupled maybe with a few agreed upon caveats where the lawyer and client agree that reasonable modifications might be necessary. Even this is substantially better than a plain "billable hour" situation.

Ultimately the idea is simple: remove the fear of a straight, unbounded billable hour arrangement, and more incremental business may come in the door. To that end, the more metrics the lawyer compiles, the more plausible and realistic the ability to offer cost certainty becomes.

I strongly suspect this approach would entice people to get to get off the sideline and call their lawyers.

THE PROBLEMS OF USING OLD-SCHOOL TIME SHEETS

Old-School Time Tracking

Recently, the folks over at <u>Above the Law</u> reported on a <u>staff nastygram</u> that was fired off by a BigLaw partner. Unfortunately, the caricature-like nature of the memo's condescending tone (that simultaneously made it both humorous and blog-worthy) overshadowed what is really an otherwise fair and important message.

Marked for distribution to folks who probably include some of the sharpest, most talented attorneys in the country (each of whom probably works ridiculously long hours), it takes a nasty temper tantrum, adds an entirely valid business concern and mixes it all up together better than your grandma's Cuisinart. It could've been closed "GOVERN YOURSELF ACCORDINGLY."

Having the luxury of distance - that is, not being one of the memo's specific targets - we can offer up a few thoughts about the substance of the message, rather than its classic form.

Obviously, when a large percentage of a firm's revenue is tied to billable hours, everyone's got to stay current on time tracking. There's no way around it, and it's really in everyone's interest to make sure time is tracked regularly and accurately. And everyone already knows this. So, what's the problem?

I don't know what particular system the firm in the memo uses for time tracking, but if the points below (which are very similar to what we've heard from several other firms) are representative of the problem - then maybe there's a different way to look at the problem rather than (just?!) berating the team:

"[Time sheets are] required to be completed on the same day as the work you do"

"Your daily time sheet should be given to your secretary BEFORE you leave for the day"

"Your secretary should input and release your time sheet"

New-School

With today's technology, a good portion of time-keeping can be handled exclusively by the attorney without the need for secretary or paralegal "input." Simple solutions are available that relegate time keeping to a passive outcome (e.g. Bill As You Work) as opposed to an active, additional job.

The more people it takes to accomplish a task, the more forms are required to be filled out, the more it becomes an independent job in and of itself - and the more likely it is to get bottlenecked behind other (often client or court-driven) priorities. With a little help from technology, the memo's generous (?!) "next-day-is-OK" exception, reserved "for those of us who also work after leaving the office" (smooooooooooooth!) might not even be required.

So - if time tracking issues are holding you back, it might make sense to consider your process, and whether there is any room for improvement or streamlining prior to going right for the staff berating memo - entertainment value notwithstanding.

CONFIDENTIAL LAW FIRM TAX PLANNING MEMO! LEAKED!

Julian Assange has nothing on us. We've been provided a copy of a super secret** tax planning memorandum from a prominent law firm. This elegantly simple yet brilliant insight just might influence your own billing practices for 2011.

***And entirely fake*

EXTREMELY CONFIDENTIAL
TO: ALL PROFESSIONALS
FROM: **Maj. Bill Fail**, Tax Chairman
DATE: January 10, 2011
SUBJECT: Tax Planning Tips

Team,

As we say goodbye to 2010, I wanted to take the opportunity to remind you that tax planning is a critically important part of our firm's operations. Each year we strive for a single planning tactic that dramatically drives down our tax liability. Last year's idea (charging our clients for services at a rate slightly below our own actual cost to provide those services, but doing so in extremely high volumes) **successfully resulted in an historic drop in our taxable income**. This year's discovery is equally exciting.

After countless of hours of advanced calculation and analysis, we're pleased to report what may be the best tax minimization plan we've uncovered in our firm's history. The successful implementation of this plan will not only result in significant tax savings, **but it will require little or no change in current workflow for many of you.**

Premised on the bedrock principle that the less revenue we bring in the less tax we pay, we surface the corollary: **The more time we write off, the more bills we write down, the more tax we avoid. It's that simple.**

You may reasonably ask: "How do we accomplish this? Our firm's professionals are among the hardest working, highest billing in the nation. We're incredibly busy helping our clients solve problems, resolve complex disputes, negotiate contracts, and we're billing more quality time than ever. Writing off time is virtually unthinkable - if anything we should be billing more!"

True, true. A sticky wicket indeed - we've found the loophole. We've solved the riddle of how we can still work hard, provide great service, yet ensure that our clients continue to discount our bills.

We looked at a sample of several successful write-downs and discounts - i.e., situations where we were able to forego payment for good work that we legitimately completed. Several clear patterns emerged, and we strongly encourage you to adopt (or for many of you, simply continue) these simple billing tactics that will most certainly keep the write-downs coming.

1. It's Just a Bill – There's No Rush to Send It

Our statisticians noticed a very strong correlation between the size of the write-off and the delay in sending the bill out. The most successful example, by far, was a solid "hide-it-under-the-desk-and-hope-it-just-goes-away-by-itself" effort by one of our litigation partners.

Waiting six months to send a client a high five-figure bill relating to depositions on a case that the client eventually lost on a summary judgment motion, resulted in nearly a 50% write-off, saving us a considerable amount in taxes!

So, next time you're ready to send out that bill, wait. Take a deep breath. Let it age like a fine wine. Resist the temptation to get trigger happy and send the bill out when the client can vividly remember all the specific work you put into the matter.

An added plus of delay - "old" bills; that is, bills that stand out as unusual often require multiple or extra levels of internal review before they can be paid.

For instance, an in-house counsel who retains our firm as litigation counsel may be able to immediately and routinely pay a bill that's within budget and contemporaneous with activity, but may need to chase down a GC, CFO or another party up the chain to get a stale bill paid - and you know they're going to have questions.

Getting our bills outside of the "pay in the ordinary course" pile can indeed promote valuable write-downs, and can also help stall our collections so **we're not faced with the pesky problem of collecting a whole bunch of cash at once.** Being overwhelmed with timely, full client payments? No, thank you.

Editor's note: This is merely 1% of the leaked data we present to you today. Tomorrow we resume with more of this letter. And it's just the tip of the iceberg!

LETTER CONTINUES....

2. Everyone Loves a Good One-Liner

Listing a single "Amount Due" on a bill (e.g. "Pay This Amount") with no accompanying explanation or detail, can also help us keep our taxable revenue down.

First, presenting a single number at the bottom of an invoice can create a kind of fun, psychological "shock and awe" for the reader. Absent an opportunity for prompt physical relief to the shock - like throwing a breakable object at one's office wall - the natural reaction often tends to be some version of "I'm not paying THAT #$%#)@ much."

Interestingly, it seems to make little difference how much the "THAT" actually is; rather, the fact that it's sitting there all alone, unexplained, in boldface type tends to ensure a strong reaction. When the immediate shock wears off, the client will predictably call and: (a) complain about the amount; and (b) demand an itemization. At that point, we're firmly on the path for a solid write-down!

Of course, the genius of sending that first bill without the accompanying detail makes sure that we implant the objection to the total amount in the client's mind before the client has a full description of what actually comprised the amount. Locking in that "write-off" bias right from the start is key to our income minimization objective.

3. Build in Solid, Time-Tested Write-Off Opportunities

Clear time itemizations and work descriptions can be problematic when trying to justify a write-off. When a client has signed an engagement letter agreeing in advance on professional service rates and is subsequently presented with a well-written, clear description of the work performed, it's much more difficult to find an opportunity to write off time.

Bills that could be read as though they are a concise summary of everything you've carefully done for your client, all the guidance, experience, and value you delivered may be good reading but it's certainly not conducive to generating valuable tax write-offs. We just can't risk collecting all that money at once.

Professionals who still use "pen-and-pencil" timekeeping, or who submit random little scribbles or voice mails to an admin, or who regularly use weekends as trips down memory lane trying to reconstruct what happened last Tuesday - these folks virtually assure us of plenty of useful write-off opportunities.

These timekeepers often rely on the multi-hour "Worked on File", "Prepared for Hearing", or "Intra-Firm Attorney Conference" descriptions which provide easy targets to justify several big red slashes through the bill. Similarly, including terms that suggest pure admin work like "downloading", "copying", "assembling" are also usually good to spark up some revenue reductions.

Resist the temptation to spend too much time accurately spelling out exactly what you did for your client, lest we collect the full amount we're due.

Unfortunately, the adoption of convenient web-based practice management tools is slowly but steadily phasing out some of these traditional, outstanding write-off opportunities (as some of you know, handling timekeeping and billing as a simple - almost passive - task, integrated with your workflow, virtually eliminates the gaps and deficiencies that we tax folks count on for our write-downs).

So, for those of you who are still using notepads, paper scraps, voice mail, or dictaphones to itemize and track your time, and who continuously endure browbeating from colleagues using today's productivity applications - take comfort. A loose description or two, a little missing time here or there, it's all helping us to open the door for a useful write-down. When your colleagues push, push back and remind them that you're doing your part to keep our firm's revenue from ramping too quickly.

For the firm's professionals who already are experiencing the convenience of a modern web-based practice management solution to facilitate your time and billing, we simply ask that you refrain from convincing your colleagues to follow your lead. While you're (selfishly) enjoying your free weekends, we tax folks will log whatever extra hours are necessary to try and deal with problems associated with the incremental cash you generate.

Let's all do our part in 2011 to continue to provide the absolute best in legal service to our clients, while making sure we keep our revenue from growing too quickly. Following even a few of these simple billing practices will go a long way toward keeping those big bill write-downs from happening and, in turn, keeping our taxable revenue down.

Regards,

Major Bill Fail

LEGAL PRODUCTIVITY
(The Sequel)

A New Productivity Measure - The Misery Index

Recently Northwestern Professor Stephen J. Harper proposed turning the standard lawyer productivity metric - average billable hours per attorney - on its head. He has some terrific points in his recent article: "A New Metric: The Misery Index."

Drawing upon analogies to DOT driving safety regulations that explicitly recognize the impact of fatigue, the Professor suggests that the measure for attorney output shouldn't be based on total hours spent; rather, it should be based on useful work product created.

The Truer Measure of Productivity

More time spent on a project does not unequivocally equal increased productivity, especially when reasonable work loads have been surpassed. In fact, as everyone knows (but few will readily admit), the complete opposite is frequently true. Spinning your wheels is still spinning your wheels, inefficiency is still inefficiency, and your 2,400th billable hour is just not as likely to be as "good" as your 1000th - whether someone is willing to pay you for it or not.

Harper proposes two indices, one for associates (AMI) and one for partners (PMI), a calculation that factors in a weighted penalty for hours billed in excess of 2,000. Ultimately it is another creative way to highlight obvious weaknesses - both of the logical and business type - in using billable hours as a measure of anything except perhaps an internal metric of actual time spent.

The Precedent of the Billable Hour

In some sense it's amazing that the billable hour has lasted as long as it has. The inertia of "precedent" - that powerful principal that gets drilled into everyone's head since the first day of law school - is definitely a factor, as is the illusion of precision offered by counting and reporting hours.

The biggest factor in the longevity of the billable hour - that is essentially a client's willingness to pay based on input rather than output - is just not going to last forever. The idea that "more billable hours" could even be thought of as a proxy for "more productivity" is going to seem absurd sooner rather than later.

One of my wise old law professors - a great practitioner who must've already been at least 120 years old back when I took his class - used to get a little twinkle in his eye and say, *"You can deem a horse a cow, but don't try to milk it."*

That pretty much sums it up.

KEY TO AN ÜBER-PRODUCTIVE + HAPPY DAY? THE NIGHT BEFORE AND THE MORNING

Time is precious, and when you engage in your activities, whether work or other, productivity is increased and stress is reduced if you have the capability of completely immersing yourself in whatever you're doing.

Flow

This state of happy productivity was termed "Flow" by a psychologist named Mihaly Csikszentmihaly (pronounced "JONES"). Flow is "a state of concentration or complete absorption with the activity at hand and the situation."

It's a beautiful thing, flow, if you can achieve it. Blocking out the stressors in your life in exchange for total immersion in your activities, whether researching, writing, conversing, exercising, or playing with kids makes you feel, well, just good.

But concentration is not easy to achieve without planning, because much of your mental state depends on how you treat your body. Without proper rest, nutrition, and blood sugar levels, it's hard to enter into flow-like states. Your mind cannot focus, you're grumpy, easily distracted, and have trouble remembering important details.

The Night Before

The key to a highly productive and satisfactory day starts the night before, with a consistent bedtime routine and schedule. Cornell University professor James Maas writes in his book <u>Power Sleep</u> that in order to maintain peak performance the next day, a bedtime routine is fundamental.

Avoiding alcohol before bedtime, reading in bed, taking a bath, and gettin' funky between the sheets (say no more!) are all great ways to induce a healthy nighttime sleep ritual.

The Morning Routine

Cut to the A.M. For busy individuals. The early morning is often the only sure-fire way to get exercise, critical for stress reduction, general health, and easier sleeping.

Likewise, since your diet is such a key part or your mental alertness, your morning routine is important to: a) ensure that you're eating a healthy breakfast and, b) pack healthy snacks with you that can sustain you all day long. A few minutes of planning in the morning, figuring out what fruits, vegetables, or other healthy options you're going to eat throughout the day do wonders for your productivity at the traditional slump times during the workday.

Suggestions of things to throw into your briefcase, or if you're an IT guy, your Darth Vader lunchbox: apples, baby carrots, yogurt, individual cottage cheese containers, bananas, and a handful of almonds. None of these are messy or nasty, they pack well, and will keep your mind sharp.

7 HIGHLY SUCCESSFUL CALENDARING HABITS FOR ATTORNEYS

Attorneys notoriously live (and die) by their calendars. Missing deadlines and hearings, I don't need to remind anyone, can result in disciplinary actions. The attorney calendar is a fine precision instrument like a car or space shuttle. It needs to be maintained, cradled, and tuned.

Done the right way, calendaring can keep you more than organized, it can improve your efficiency and even help ensure a sane work life balance. Keeping these seven guidelines in mind can make a big difference.

1) Keep to-do's separate from calendar entries.

David Allen's GTD fans are familiar with his idea of separating to-do items with calendar entries. His advice: only put something on a calendar if it has a date associated with it. Don't schedule something with the idea that you'll work on it that day. Allen writes in Getting Things Done:

The calendar should be sacred territory. If you write something there, it must get done that day or not at all. The only rewriting should be for changed appointments.

2) Always maintain critical information in calendar appointments.

The last thing you need in your hectic day is looking at a calendar event, then shuffling to another program to find telephone numbers, contact information, or relevant details for your appointment. When you schedule the event, put phone numbers in the event header field so you don't even have to drill into the calendar information for details.

Relevant URLS, notes, and directions should also be stored in the metadata for the event (i.e. notes and location fields).

3) Bill directly from your calendar entries if your software permits.

Your time entry is automated if you use a calendar program that automatically funnels the duration of your appointment into your billing program. Not all calendaring programs do this, so investigate which ones do.

It's not just hourly billers who need to track time. Studying time spent on flat fee and contingency cases gives you an idea of the ROI for your efforts. Furthermore, should the court require you to provide time-records, you're covered.

Shameless plug and full disclosure: Rocket Matter, the author's company, provides this Bill as You Work functionality. We observed real-world attorneys spending days recreating their invoices by pouring over their calendars and thought that was an inefficient and unprofitable way to do things.

4) Be as mobile as possible.

You need to be able to quickly check and make appointments whenever and wherever you are. With smartphones and near-ubiquitous Internet access, there's no excuse not to be able to know and update your calendar. If your calendaring software isn't mobile, hopefully it can interact with a fully portable offering like Google Calendar.

5) Limit recurring events as much as possible.

There are certainly exceptions to this rule. Status meetings are a biggie. At our workplace we put biweekly review and retrospective meetings on our calendars.

We don't however, put our daily standup on the calendar. That would clutter things up. You want a calendar that tells you something interesting not a bunch of noisy information. When you do something everyday, you don't need a reminder that it's going to occur unless you're Guy Pierce's character from "Memento".

Also, eliminate any meeting on your calendar that you don't follow through with more often than not. Any regular appointments that you don't regularly hit? Kill them and free the space.

6) Review your calendar nightly and weekly.

Most likely, your calendar is in front of you all day long. But two things will put your mind at ease when you break from work: Make sure you scan the following day's events before you leave work at night, in addition, scan it before the weekend's over on Sunday night.

Knowing what's ahead not only helps you avoid missing early morning appointments, it gives you a sense of peace and control knowing that tomorrow is well-planned.

7) Use time blocking for personal priorities.

If you have to be somewhere, be it the gym for exercise, visiting your bank, or seeing your kid's dance recital - block it off! If it's your goal to go to the driving range on Mondays at six, block off that time in advance and make it happen. Don't hesitate to put a hard stop on your time.

3 SENTENCE EMAILS MEAN MORE BILLABLE TIME FOR ATTORNEYS

Email is a personal scourge of mine, as I presume it is for most busy professionals. I'd rather be talking to customers, writing blog posts, coming up with our next great Snuggie® promotion, or some other odd thing I do during the business day.

For lawyers, getting sucked into an email morass can be a black hole for profits, considering the billable hour nature of legal work.

The 3 Sentence Email

Enter the three sentence email, a meme which has been circulating around tech circles. The whole idea is spelled out elegantly on the site three.sentenc.es, and advocates responses of three sentences or less, much like an SMS message.

Not only does this practice reduce the amount of time you spend composing your emails, it reduces the amount of time reading emails for your recipients. And if the whole world embraces three sentence emails, then we'll all spend a lot less time reading email.

An article on TechCrunch on this subject offers up some alarming time-sucking statistics about email usage:

The inbox has become the "dreaded inbox" for so many people. A recent study by Xobni claimed 1 in 5 Americans check emails either as the first thing they do in the morning or the last thing at night. 26% of Americans feel they can't handle or feel overwhelmed by the number of emails they receive during vacation. Another report by The Radicati Group says the typical corporate user sends 36 emails and receives 61 legitimate emails during the average day. An IDC study estimates email consumes an average of 13 hours per week per information worker.

Three sentence emails, combined with Paul Burton's QuietSpacing techniques on email usage that we learned about in our last webinar, give me at least a sense of control over my inbox so it doesn't spill over and bite enormous chunks out of the rest of my day.

But here's the important part: you must spread the word, so we're all reading short itty-bitty emails.

HOW TO ACHIEVE EMAIL NIRVANA

You may have read <u>the earlier article about email batching</u>- a technique that helps you conquer the day's email once or twice a day, rather than being bogged down in constant responses. This time, I'm going to discuss a different but complementary technique: Inbox Nirvana.

Before I do that, though, I did get some feedback from people on the <u>first article about email batching</u>. I understand that it's hard to cut down on checking your email. Even I can't do it all the time, because I know how stimulating it is to get an email.

If you can't cut down all the way, go to once an hour. Keep your notifications off and check at a set time. Again, the earlier rule applies - if once an hour is not soon enough, the sender will call you or find another way to reach you.

Welcome to the Four Steps to Email Nirvana

Step One

Email batching, as previously discussed, is the first step to Email Nirvana.

Step Two

Step two is unsubscribing. If you're getting advertisements, newsletters, Twitter updates, LinkedIn messages, and Facebook notifications hundreds of times a day, you're wasting time. Click unsubscribe on the newsletters (unless they're from <u>Rocket Matter</u>) and advertisements (and make sure you're sending SPAM to your junk folder). Tell Twitter, LinkedIn, and Facebook to stop notifying you - and download HootSuite or Tweetdeck if it's imperative you receive updates. I use Tweetdeck to manage over 40 columns of constantly updating information from Twitter, Facebook, Buzz, LinkedIn, FourSquare, and more - and none of it is in my email.

Step Three

Step three of Email Nirvana is getting your inbox clear. Email Nirvana subscribes to the theory that inbox emptiness is next to godliness. Once a week, set aside time to ensure that every email receives the attention that it deserves: file old messages in an archive folder, move bills and invoices to an invoice folder, separate client documents to client folders, and so forth.

Step Four

Step four may be a bit difficult. Business email should be business email. Keep personal email out of it. Lawyers should know this instinctively, but your company email is generally not private, so try to keep business email to the business. Do make sure that your emails are straightforward and to the point. I liked to write in-depth, pleasant email until someone asked why I was upset with them when I sent a three-word email one day. Since that day, I make sure my professional emails are as straightforward and polite as possible.

There's one additional step that can be taken if you're absolutely overwhelmed, although it is not the best idea for lawyers who may be relying on their inbox. It will get you to Email Nirvana immediately and it involves the Delete key. Send a message to everyone in your inbox telling them you've lost your email... then hit delete on every message in your inbox. The important messages will be resent - but now you should know how to keep on top of them!

Jerry Levine is an attorney, social media evangelist, technologist, and all-around awesome guy. He consults with FSRDG (www.fsrdg.com), a legal technology, eDiscovery, and investment firm; founded NetworkEsq. to speak about social media and social networking, and edits the Journal of Legal Technology Risk Management (www.ltrm.org), as well as few other concepts that are still brewing. Outside of law, Jerry likes food, brewing his own beer, playing with his Wii, and has two cats - Lo Mein & Yakineko. He can be reached at jerry@jerrylevine.com, on the web at jerrylevine.com, and is @jerry_levine on twitter.

Dumpster Day: Make your Law Office a Less Cluttered And Happier Place to Work

We've been extolling the virtues of David Allen's GTD® system for years, devoting an entire chapter to it in our e-Book, Legal Productivity. However, one of the ingredients in the GTD system that we haven't mentioned even once is Dumpster Day.

Dumpster Day is exactly what you might suspect (unless you're confusing it with Dumpster Diving, a uniquely disgusting American tradition where high school kids obtain amounts of stale donuts from a Dunkin Donuts dumpster). It's a day dedicated to cleaning out the office.

Allen writes in Getting Things Done:

Employees get to come to work in sneakers and jeans, put their phones on do-not-disturb, and get current with their stored items.

Clutter has a huge affect on mood. According to Gretchin Rubin, author of The Happiness Project, "One of the most striking things I've discovered since starting my happiness project is the influence of clutter on mood. For most people, outer order contributes to inner calm; a messy coat closet, for instance, is clearly a very trivial element in life, yet clearing out that messy coat closet gives a disproportionately large happiness boost."

So make an event of it. Everyone is encouraged to go through their desks, files, bookshelves, and purge themselves of stuff they don't need anymore. If there's any doubt, toss it.

Do you really need the lanyard from the convention you went to in aught five? How about the book on Internet marketing you haven't cracked once?

For books, old electronics, and other items that might have value to someone else, it helps to set up a banquet table where employees can discard those items and potentially find something that they might need.

As we head into the renewal period, as well as the slow end-of-the-year business period, shed some office crud. And get your whole staff to join in.

Why Law Firms Should Embrace Cycles: Getting Organized is One Thing, Staying Organized is Another

On my last post of 2010, <u>I discussed how the overriding theme I spot in personal happiness, productivity, and self-help literature is getting organized</u>, that leads to less stress and better execution.

One commenter wrote that with all of the spinning plates he has as a solo attorney, it's nearly impossible to carve out time to become more organized. When you have a living, breathing, belching machine of a law firm, it's tough to step back and take a look and come up with suggested adjustments to your operations, much less execute on your observations.

Getting Organized

To this fellow, I suggest taking a look at the Agile Retrospective meeting, which I wrote about in <u>ILTA's White Paper on Legal Project Management</u>. You hold a Retrospective with your staff every two weeks or a month for 30 minutes (have them come in early if you *have* to), and you make a list of what to Start doing, what to Stop doing, and what to Continue doing.

At the very least, the Retrospective minimally interrupts the office and forces you to see the organizations and processes comprising your law office.

And you don't have to execute all your changes at once. Pick a couple, or even one that might have the most impact and free up some resources. Maybe it's time to get that <u>easy-</u>

to-learn online legal practice management software you've been looking at. :-)

Think of it like you're backed up to your own end zone and you need a little breathing room.

From there, regular Retrospective meetings will be easier and give you more material that you can sink your teeth into.

Staying Organized with Cycles

It's one thing to get organized, and it's another thing to stay organized, as all of us who have made resolutions are painfully aware. The universe trends towards entropy. So does your desk drawer and wallet. And since it takes so much energy to get organized in the first place, it's a total waste to let yourself slip backwards towards chaos once you've achieved order.

Hence the nature of cycles. The reason the Agile Retrospective is so effective is because it happens on a recurring basis. The GTD weekly review gives peace of mind because it cleans out the psyche once a week.

So my suggestion to stay organized is to embrace cycles. Here's a good gauge of activities which will keep your mind crisp and uncluttered, ready to handle the barrage of insanity that invades the small law office on a daily basis:

1) Once a week: Weekly Review

2) Once a week: Clear off your desk

3) Once every two weeks: Retrospective meeting .

4) Once a month: Clean out your wallet.

5) Once every two months: Clean out your closet and desk drawers.

ADDITIONAL RESOURCES

4 Resources to Create Amazing Attorney Websites

Let's assume, for a second, that your law firm has a website (your law firm has a website, right?) The question then become, is your website earning its keep?

That's a tough question. At the very least, your website should tell the world what you do, hopefully start persuading your audience to take a closer look at you, and possibly engage and get found with a search engine.

That's a lot of stuff, and website optimization, both for search engines and audiences can be daunting for busy attorneys. So for this reason, here are three quick resources that can help you get started:

1) Other Great Website Examples

Take a look at other great attorney websites and understand what makes them effective. Attorney at Work recently profiled 5 websites, discussing why each one was a "Winning Website".

2) Website Grader

Run your site through Website Grader, built and maintained by Hubspot, a leader in inbound marketing. Website Grader will give your site a number grade out of a hundred and make suggestions about what you can do better.

3) Free Webinars

Check out the resources from our free webinar, Ten Steps to Building Winning Websites, with Internet marketer Jay

Berkowitz of Ten Golden Rules. Jay packs more information than you can imagine into his hour presentations, and it should give you some ideas to consider.

4) Customizing Services

Take a look at Headway, built by blogger Grant Griffiths. Headway is a very slick do-it-yourself wrapper around the popular blogging platform Wordpress. The tools for search engine optimization are solid and it features clever ways to build your site to maintain the same look and feel of your logo (your law firm has a logo, right?).

5 GREAT FREE RESOURCES FOR SOLO AND SMALL LAW FIRM ATTORNEYS

"The best things in life are free. But you can keep 'em for the birds and bees."

So sang Barret Strong originally, followed by dozens of other cover artists including The Beatles, later. But as it turns out, there's a lot of free stuff these days, that had Mr. Strong known about, may have changed his lyrics.

If you're running a small law firm and are looking for some advice on the cheap, take a look at these great resources which you may or may not know about:

1) SCORE.org

The SCORE organization has nothing to do with what happens after you round third base. Rather, it's wisdom from retired business professionals free of charge, to you. You, as a business owner, can be paired with a former company head to serve as a mentor. In addition, the SCORE website has some terrific financial spreadsheets which can help you assemble your balance sheet, income, and cash flow statements.

2) MILO

MILO, which stands for Macs in Law Offices, is arguably the most cutting-edge legal technology community around. MILO runs a listserv you can sign up for, an annual conference, and a monthly podcast. Even if you're not a Mac, iPad, or iPhone aficionado, the experts weighing in on the MILO list serve are some of the most knowledgeable around when it comes to paperless law firms, web applications, or electronics.

3) PMA's

Practice Management Advisors, or PMAs, are employed by bar associations around the U.S. and Canada to advise their constituents on best practices for running, or in sad cases, shutting down a law firm. Need a recommendation for software or business practices? Call the PMA for your jurisdiction. They can assist in understanding the confusing world of trust accounting. Check here for a list of PMAs.

4) SOLOSEZ

SOLOSEZ is an ABA listserv, but like MILO, transcends email and is actually a thriving community for solo and small firm attorneys. The conversation ranges from legal issues to technology to casual introductions and banters. New members introduce themselves by mentioning their favorite mixed drinks. And SEZZERS, as members are called, often meet-up at conventions and cities around the country.

5) ABA LTRC

Any technology question you possibly have can be answered by the ABA's Legal Technology Resource Center, or LTRC. According to their mission statement on their website, "The ABA's Legal Technology Resource Center's expert staff helps lawyers understand and use technology successfully, so they can focus on providing the highest quality legal services to their clients or organizations."

Those are our suggestions, among many of amazing free resources in our Internet age. What are your highly recommended free resources?

FIND OUT MORE

By reading Part One of *The Law Firm of Tomorrow*, **you're already at the vanguard of the legal profession.** In Part Two, we'll explore more powerful business practices and take a look at how you're handling cash. In Part Three, we'll go deeper into everyday work habits for a more efficient office.

Please take a look at more great resources:

Understanding Social Media for Legal Professionals

Understanding Cloud Computing for Legal Professionals

The Legal Productivity Blog

From RocketCLE:

Learn the Hottest Apps for Lawyers

Ten Steps To Building & Promoting Law Firm Websites

Rocket Matter Product Information:

Sign up for a free Rocket Matter product demonstration.

Attend a free Rocket Matter training class.

www.ingramcontent.com/pod-product-compliance
Lightning Source LLC
Chambersburg PA
CBHW022000170526
45157CB00003B/1072